Print-on-Demand Book Publishing

A New Approach to Printing and Marketing Books for Publishers and Authors

Foner Books
Springfield, MA

Morris Rosenthal

Please Read

The author has done his best to present accurate and up-to-date information in this book, but he cannot guarantee that the information is correct or will suit your particular situation. This book is sold with the understanding that the publisher and the author are not engaged in rendering legal, accounting or any other professional services. If expert assistance is required, the services of a competent professional should be sought.

Copyright 2004 Morris Rosenthal
ISBN 0-9723801-3-2

Editor: Tracie Shea

Copy Editor: Anne Stewart

Proofreaders: Franklyn Dailey Jr., Henry Foner and The Rosenthals

Published by Foner Books
www.fonerbooks.com

Contents

Introduction

A variety of changes in business practices and advances in technology are blurring the boundary between authoring and publishing. The new reality is an absolute explosion of new titles released, over 150,000 per year in the U.S. alone. New technologies in book production allow for smaller quantities of books to be printed, which translates for publishers into lower financial commitments on new titles. Another part of the equation is the rise of the super-store book chains, with the capacity to shelve five to ten times as many books as a traditional bookstore. The computerization of book production allows publishers to run virtual operations, with staffing concentrated in marketing and legal departments. An author submits a manuscript as a standard word processor file, which the publisher then e-mails to a chain of freelance editors, proofreaders and layout-artists, and finally to a printer in another country with low production costs.

An unfortunate side effect of the modernization of the book industry has been a perceptible reduction in the quality of books. Even the most prestigious trade imprints are producing books marred by repeated phrases and other errors typical of on-screen copy editing, word processor auto-correction and spell checks. Corner cutting on basic quality issues such as paper stock and production quality puts authors at odds with their publishers, whose only explanation is "competitive pressures." Author royalties and advances fall as publishers, desperate to show profit growth, cut anywhere they can and introduce ever more new titles in search of elusive economies of scale. Online booksellers have changed the economics of the remainder and used book markets in a way that most publishers have yet to acknowledge or begin to address.

For all the doom and gloom, these same technological advancements have also brought about unprecedented new opportunities for authors and publishers alike. The Internet has brought writers an indispensable new way to reach vast audiences and promote published books. This has much greater impact on the book business than technological advances in publisher workflow, but has been largely ignored by most authors and publishers. The new pre-press software allows a skilled operator working on a home PC to produce the electronic files for printing books that are indistinguishable from the best the trades have to offer. Print-on-demand allows publishers to print commercially competitive books a single copy at a time, a true revolution in the basic publishing model. The very newness of these innovations ensures that no one is currently using them all to the best possible effect. This means there is more opportunity than ever for new authors and publishers to break into the business.

Revolutionary new technologies often meet limited success at their initial introduction because they are forced to operate in the mode of a technology they are replacing. At the beginning of World War One, the German Navy deployed submarines, known as U-boats (for Undersea Boats) against merchant shipping. A U-boat would lurk underwater in shipping lanes, waiting for its prey. Then, in the best tradition of naval warfare, it would surface, hail the surprised merchant vessel and give the crew time to launch lifeboats before destroying the ship with a torpedo or shells from a deck gun. The allied countermeasures included arming some merchant vessels with sufficient weaponry to sink a submarine, and the Germans were forced to change their tactics to remaining underwater and firing torpedoes from ambush on unsuspecting ships, which became known as "unrestricted warfare." Looking back on it now, stealth seems like the obvious model for submarine warfare, but the Germans had started by applying this new technology to the old surface navy model and ended up losing many submarines and crews at the war's beginning, viewed by some historians as a critical error.

We'll examine print-on-demand publishing in the context of traditional publishing models and as a unique new model which has come into its own with the Internet. While the processes followed in preparing new titles for traditional publication on offset presses can also be applied to POD, it's critical to realize that there are other paths. The traditional publishing process evolved over hundreds of years, dedicated to making the peculiar economics of that industry feasible. POD does not obey the economics of traditional offset publishing, though many publishers have been slow to realize this. This book is written for both authors and publishers who wish to take advantage of the unique possibilities of POD, as opposed to simply using it to keep old books in print.

Publisher Basics

Anybody who prints a bunch of pages on their PC printer, punches holes in the margin and arranges them in a three-ring binder is perfectly free to write "A Book – Published by Me" on the cover and call themselves a publisher. If they keep track of their expenses, sell these books, and file Federal and State taxes as a publisher, then they really are a publisher. But that's not the definition we're going to use in this book, and it's not the definition book stores, distributors or printers use. As far as the industry is concerned, a publisher is a person or business entity who has purchased at least one ISBN (International Standard Book Number) block.

ISBN and BowkerLink

The U.S. ISBN agency is operated by Bowker in a stewardship arrangement. In addition, Bowker publishes the encyclopedic "Books in Print" directory, which lists all books with an active ISBN (meaning those which haven't been officially declared out of print). The ISBN is the only number you must have for your book to be uniquely identifiable throughout the world, making it possible for people to walk into a bookstore and order it. Well, that's how it's supposed to work. In practice, bookstores want to order books through their usual channels. If your book, uniquely identified by its ISBN, isn't available through any of their regular distributors, they need to look up the publisher information in "Books in Print" and attempt to order direct. Most bookstores will only do this for a very persistent customer. They may demand prepayment and charge the customer an additional fee for the special order, because customers frequently fail to return to purchase special order books. Small publishers with limited or no distribution will receive the occasional fax or surface mail purchase order for a book, asking that the book be sent to them post-haste with an invoice. There's only a reasonable chance the invoice will ever get paid. In other words, an ISBN block makes a publisher, but it's not a publishing business unless the publisher has a way to attract customers and sell them books.

ISBN blocks can be purchased from Bowker online or through the mail, and for an extra fee you can expedite the process if you're in a really big hurry. The basic costs as of January 2004 were:

Size of block	Registration	Additional
10	$225	$14.95
100	$800	$37.95
1,000	$1,200	$119.95
10,000	$3,000	$299.95

You can go to their website with a credit card and order online at either:

http://www.bowker.com or http://www.isbn.org

or mailing:

> U.S. ISBN Agency
> 630 Central Avenue
> New Providence, NJ 07974
> Tel: 877-310-7333
> Fax: 908-219-0188
> isbn-san@bowker.com

Once an ISBN block has been assigned, the online BowkerLink site is the best way to manage those numbers, create new titles, make corrections to title or publisher information or take books out of print. Registration for BowkerLink is free, but there is a learning curve to using the interface, which is one of the balkiest pieces of software you could ever hope to meet. Make sure you save your changes when you complete a registration session, which the software will do only if it's satisfied with the way you filled out the blanks.

The ISBN should always be included on the book cover as a barcode on the back, which enables distributors and retail stores to move the book in and out of inventory with a standard barcode scanner, like all retail products. If you do not include the barcode in your cover design, distributors will charge you for "stickering" the book, creating a barcode sticker with the correct ISBN to allow tracking. The ISBN is actually embedded in a Bookland EAN (European Article Number), and you aren't required to include the price in the coding, though it's a good idea to do so. If a book is destined for sales in nontraditional outlets, you should also include a UPC (Universal Product Code), which is suited for general merchandise. The Bookland barcode for this book was obtained for free online at:

http://www.cgpp.com/bookland/isbn.html

Copyright

According to "Circular 1 – Copyright Basics," published by the United States Copyright Office: "Copyright protection subsists from the time the work is created in fixed form. The copyright in the work of authorship *immediately* becomes the property of the author who created the work. Only the author or those deriving their rights through the author can rightfully claim copyright." That's a three sentence quote out of a 12 page document, but it expresses the critical concept of copyright protection. When an author creates a work, that author immediately benefits from a certain level of copyright protection.

So why register your work with the government and pay a fee? Creating a work in fixed form is one thing, and proving in a court of law when you actually created that work is another. Also, if you ever find yourself in a court battle over copyright infringement, having registered a copyright within three months of publication allows you to recover attorney's fees and statutory damages.

Published books should contain a visual notice of copyright (registration is not required to include this notification) that consists of three elements. The first element is the symbol, word, or abbreviation for copyright:

©, Copyright or Copr. The second element is the year the work was first published, or the year a collection or compilation was first published, in cases where portions of the work were previously published. The third element is the name of the copyright owner. The example from the title page of this book is "Copyright 2004 Morris Rosenthal."

Everybody involved in publishing, whether or not they have a lawyer on retainer, should read the Copyright Basics circular at least once. You can request a free printed copy from the U.S. Copyright Office, or you can download an electronic copy in PDF format which can be read and printed with the free Adobe Acrobat reader. Actual instructions for which form you need to fill out (short and long forms, just like taxes) and the forms themselves are also available online in PDF format. Most book publishers work primarily with Form TX or Short Form TX.

The copyright fee as of January 2004 was $30, payable by check or money order, and you must submit two copies of a published work or one copy of an unpublished work along with the completed application. The Copyright Office website address is:

http://www.copyright.gov

or mailing:

Library of Congress
Copyright Office
Publications Section LM-455
101 Independence Avenue, S.E.
Washington, D.C. 20559-6000
(202) 707-3000

Library of Congress and CIP

A Library of Congress Control Number (LCCN) is not necessary for publishing a book, and indeed, this book doesn't carry an LC control number. A more useful number can sometimes be obtained before publication from the Cataloging in Publication (CIP) division of the Library of Congress, but the program excludes self-publishers and many small publishers. The CIP is useful for librarians to easily catalog a newly acquired book, so if your book is intended for a primarily academic audience or if you expect large library sales, you can try to get a number direct from CIP (depends on the mood of the employee assigned to your account). Another option is to pay a local librarian or an Internet service a few dollars to generate a PCIP (Publishers Cataloging in Publication) number for you. However, there's nothing official about a PCIP number; you can even generate one yourself. It's just a courtesy to librarians, some of whom will ignore it and create a cataloging number themselves. Some publishers claim that a genuine CIP number has an effect on sales, but I've not seen it myself. Small publisher library sales come primarily through library patrons requesting the book, at which point it makes no difference whether the book has a cataloging number.

Book Printing

The traditional method of printing books is through an offset press, so-called because the image of the pages being printed is transferred from an inked plate to an intermediate roller which actually inks the paper. Large offset presses are called web presses, cost millions of dollars, and are fed by huge rolls of paper. A medium size web press prints sixteen pages of standard book formats at a time, eight pages per side, known as "8-up." Whatever the actual number of printed pages in a book, the publisher will be charged for a number of pages that's an exact multiple of 16, which results in blank pages at the end of the book. Smaller offset presses are sheet fed and can produce books with a lower multiple of pages if they print 17" x 11" stock, room for four 5.5" x 8.5" pages, a standard paperback size, or "4-up." The minimum number of pages that are printed at a time by offset presses, either eight or sixteen pages, are folded together in a unit called a "signature" and bound into books.

Print-on-demand printers, essentially hyper-fast, roll fed laser printers, also print a number of pages at a time, which are then cut down to the actual page size in the book. Some POD printers require that books contain a number of pages divisible by four. Unlike offset printing, which is an inking process, POD lasers use a toner process, like an office laser printer or copying machine. The toner process, particularly at lower resolutions on high-speed printers, does not produce as high a quality image as a properly run offset press. This may change in the future, but for the time being, commercial POD printing is not recommended for books with a significant amount of photographs or grey scale artwork. In the case of both POD and offset printing, color interiors are more expensive than black and white, but with POD printing, the cost difference is currently prohibitive.

Book Binding

Binding is a critical stage of the book production process; in fact, it's really the step that differentiates between a pile of paper and a book. While there are only two basic types of books, paperback and hardcover, there are a number of binding techniques in use. The standard paperback is usually "perfect bound," a process which involves grinding smooth the binding surface of the book, impregnating it with glue, and wrapping a thicker paper stock cover around it. Paperback covers for both offset and POD books are usually printed in full color (requires a mix of four colors of ink or toner) and are often printed on stock that's coated on one side for a glossy appearance.

Some paperbacks are intended to be laid flat, like many cookbooks and hobby how-to's, and these work best with spiral bindings. True hard covers, often referred to as "cloth," have the signatures sewn together into a book through a piece of cloth, after which the hard cover is glued over the strong end papers. Many offset printers and most POD printers also offer case bindings, sometimes called library bindings, because libraries frequently send out paperback books to be rebound as hard covers for greater endurance. The perfect bound book is glued into a hardcover, and classy binders add fake cloth crowns to the binding, to make them look like they were sewn. Case bound hard covers open stiffer than sewn books and probably don't last through nearly as many readings.

Most hardcover books are finished with a dust jacket, a full color wrap that is folded around the book covers but not glued into place. The inside flaps of the dust jacket are traditionally used to give a brief summary of the book and a biography of the author. If the designer makes the flaps too long, they tend to curl up when the book is open and quickly get crumpled. Trade publishers will always order a number of dust jackets far exceeding the number of books printed, so they can "refresh" bookstore returns with a new dust jacket.

Inventory

Inventory is product that a business purchases for stock in hopes of selling it in the near future. Books, as an inventory product, present certain problems for large and small publishers alike. First, they are heavy and take up a lot of space. Even when a book has a proven sales record, ordering in quantity to obtain the best pricing can turn out to be more costly in the long run. Consider a small hardcover or medium size paperback book in quantity 10,000, where either book weighs approximately one pound. That's 10,000 pounds of books, or five tons. In order to get a reasonable shipping cost, five tons of books will be shipped on palettes (forklift skids) in a semi-trailer, which requires a loading dock and a forklift to unload the books. Even if you rent or borrow a small truck to pick up the books yourself, you're talking about a lot of trips back and forth and around 200 boxes of books weighing 50 pounds each. Stored books are subject to environmental damage such as humidity, and until they get sold, it's money that isn't available for further business operations.

Print-on-demand solves the inventory problem, and some would argue that this is POD's strongest merit. With Lightning Source and a few other POD printers who will handle distribution and drop shipping (shipping orders direct to customers), the publisher doesn't need to carry any inventory at all. At least one shipping leg, from the printer to the publisher, is totally eliminated, and there's no shipping charge for books supplied into distribution. No money is tied-up in inventory, and there are never any unsold boxes of books stacked up at the end of a title's life. There's no need for the publisher to pay for warehouse space or convert the basement into book storage, run several dehumidifiers, and hope it doesn't flood.

Publishers who want to continue selling books direct, as we do, can order smaller quantities than are possible with offset printing. We never order more than 25 copies of a title at a time, primarily to reduce our inventory to what can fit on a table top. Since it usually takes less than a week for our printer to fill orders, from the moment we submit the order on the web to the arrival of UPS at our door, we can confidently run a mail order sales operation with just a week's worth of books on hand. The padded book shipping envelopes, which we order in quantity 100 to get the price under $0.30 each, take up more space in the shipping area than the books do!

Expenses and Write-offs

The IRS (Internal Revenue Service) makes some allowances for the limited bookkeeping and capital of small publishers, as compared to midsize and large trade publishers. The last time I spoke to an IRS agent, I was told that a publisher with under $1,000,000 a year in sales didn't have to follow strict accrual accounting for each new product (book). Large publishers are required to associate every expense that goes into the production of a title with that title only, and can deduct those expenses only against the profits from that title. If that title fails to generate more profits than expenses, eventually the publisher can take the loss against the overall profits of the company, but it's not a "whatever you feel like" process. With no capital costs to depreciate, we've been able to account for all of our business activities on a single Schedule C.

Expenses and write-offs often sound like good things when explained by an accountant, since they lower the amount of tax you have to pay. Unfortunately, to generate expenses and write-offs, you have to take money out of your pocket. For example, I attended a government sponsored conference on E-books in Washington, DC a few years ago. The conference cost a few hundred dollars, the hotel cost a few hundred dollars, the tolls and gas for the 800 mile trip added up to something, for a total cost of around $700. At the end of the year, I was happy to deduct this expense from my business, saving me around $250 on my taxes. Unfortunately, I didn't generate any useful business contacts at the conference nor could I apply the knowledge to any profitable venture, so in essence, I spent $700 to save $250.

Author Basics

Every new author who starts writing a book without a contract in hand is faced with the same problem once it's complete: how to get published. Authors with the foresight to start promoting a book before it's completed will have an easier time finding a trade publisher, assuming their promotional success doesn't convince them to try publishing themselves. Websites and POD books can both serve as stepping stones into a trade publishing contract, replacing the traditional entrees of newspaper journalism and magazine writing. Perhaps one of the reasons that websites remain an absent or underutilized tool in the aspiring author's portfolio is that they rarely pay immediate returns, as do newspapers and magazines. What's unique about the Internet for new writers is that there are no gatekeepers. The collective web community decides the value of your contributions on the merits, by either coming or staying away, and there are more potential readers than you could reach with any other medium. If you have something to say, the odds are in your favor. The Internet is a tool that takes time to master, but the more you invest, the more you'll get out.

There's always room in the publishing industry for a few best selling authors whose agents and editors work full time to insulate them from harshness of the publishing business climate, but if you're reading this book, you probably aren't one of them. Authors who sit back and trust in their publisher to take care of the business side of publishing will most likely end up both broke and unemployed. Publishers who quote "competitive pressures" but fail to alter their basic business model in response to those pressures will end up joining their former authors on the unemployment line. Unlike every other media involved in publishing, the Internet is a two way street, where book promotion and reader feedback take place on the same page. If you're writing just to please yourself, then go ahead and finish what you're working on before worrying about what you're going to do with it. If you're writing as a business, you had better invest significant time in making sure that there's a market for your next book and that you have a proven way to reach to that market before you settle down to serious writing.

Query Letters and Book Proposals

Most publishers expect the book proposal process to begin with a query letter or e-mail, briefly stating what a proposed book is about, who the market is and why you're the author to write it. Publishers are more likely to actually read query letters than anything else you send precisely because they're short, so it's important to come across as a professional. Nonfiction publishers will take query letters seriously, even from unpublished authors, if they're persuasive and to the point. Let's say you want to write a book about being an American and you're looking to find a trade publisher willing to pay you an advance. The surest way to get your query letter thrown out is to write, "The market for this book is the nearly 300 million Americans, plus the six billion or so foreigners who either love or hate us." That's not a market, it's all of mankind. Books about being American are published and sold every year, and they all have a target audience. It could be a high school civics book, a grammar school reader, a manual for gun-toting survivalists or an apology for liberals. No sober acquisitions editor is going to believe you can write a book that will suit all these audiences. Even if you've written the next "Huckleberry Finn," you had better propose that the book will be attractive to young readers who live near water if you want to be taken seriously.

Whole books have been published on the subject of writing query letters and book proposals, and when it's appropriate to combine the two. A query letter, and more recently, a query e-mail, is a quick check on whether or not an acquisitions editor at a publisher has any interest in publishing a title in the genre and topic you're writing about. In terms of length, don't go over one page in a query letter or two paragraphs in a query e-mail, and in both cases, get the basic book idea into the first few sentences. If you know that a particular acquisitions editor is actively acquiring books in your field, you can skip the query letter and send a proposal, but it should still get right to the point. Don't include sample chapters in an unsolicited proposal; it's not professional and the bulk may keep anybody at the publisher from bothering to open the envelope. Enclosing a Self Addressed Stamped Envelope (SASE) is a matter of taste, your phone number and an e-mail address are critical. Some acquisitions editors see SASE as the mark of the amateur or an invitation to rejection, while old school editors may be put off if you don't include it. Many of today's editors are more likely to pick up the phone or send an e-mail than to play post office.

The purpose of a query letter is to hook editors, and the job of the proposal is to reel them in. The book proposal size is inversely proportional to the fame of the author, so that an unknown author usually has to submit a completed manuscript (particularly in fiction) to be considered for publication while a big name may receive a contract for a concept. A description of the proposed book, including an outline or sample chapters, is almost incidental to a modern book proposal. The main challenge is to present a compelling case as to why a new book in the given genre, by the particular author, with a certain subject, will succeed in the market. Critical components of a proposal include: how the author will promote the book, an analysis of the strengths and weaknesses of competing books, and what credentials the author brings to the table, either previous success as an author or name recognition in a professional field. Few continuously employed acquisitions editors have the authority or courage to publish a book just because it's well-written.

There's not even a discussion anymore over whether or not it's ethical to send query letters out to multiple publishers simultaneously. It is. Some old fashioned writers hesitate to send a full proposal to more that one publisher at a time, and some old fashioned editors will become indignant if you do. Just ask an acquisitions editor if they'll agree not to consider any other books while they're thinking about yours and see what you get for an answer. When a book proposal reaches the point of serious consideration, i.e., the acquisitions editor you contacted asks for more information and starts talking about presenting it to an editorial board, you can tell them if the book is being seriously considered by another publisher. Keep in mind that it's impossible to get offers from competing publishers without proposing the book to them, and competing offers are the only real way you can discover the market value of a manuscript.

Protecting Ideas and Negotiating

One question that frequently comes up in discussions with unpublished writers is, "How do I get the publisher to sign an Non-Disclosure Agreement (NDA) before telling them about my idea?" You don't, or at least I've never heard of it happening. When you send out a query letter or a proposal, particularly in nonfiction, you're taking a chance that your ideas will be stolen, but it's a long shot. Some unethical editors may use book proposals for idea mining or even pass the ideas on to favored authors, but I don't believe it happens all that often. On the other side of the coin, I was recently asked by an editor to commit to a contract or informal agreement early in the negotiation process, before he would tell me what direction he wanted to go with a book I'd written, lest I take his valuable ideas elsewhere. I pointed out to him that neither the copyright office nor the patent office put any stock in "ideas," and that the value is in the implementation, the writing, in the case of a book. I also got a good laugh out of it. Publishers are never shy about asking authors for favors that they'd never grant themselves.

If you aren't willing to walk away from the table without a deal, you're not negotiating, you're begging. New authors may think they have absolutely no muscle in negotiations, particularly if they've followed the "one publisher at a time" approach. Any time you can talk to a publisher with both of you knowing that another publisher is in the wings, you're going to get a better deal. However, even if you only have one publisher interested and it's your first book, you still have a little bit of bargaining strength based on the fact that they believe they can make a profit by signing you. It's important to realize that the standard contract offered by publishers isn't standard at all. It's just what they happen to be offering new authors that month. If they want to publish your book, they aren't going to lose interest because you ask for a minor change in some contract language that's expressly unfavorable to you. They might say "No," but negotiating contracts is their business and they won't take your asking as an insult. Any publisher that acts offended if you consult a lawyer has something to hide.

Agents and Lawyers

Whether or not all writers should hire agents is always a hot topic of debate amongst authors. There are some fields, such as literary fiction, where an agent may be necessary just to get a book considered. Most of the big trade publishers who once employed readers to look at potential new titles now rely exclusively on agents to bring in book ideas and manuscripts. If you have the fame or the confidence to believe that your novel has a chance at being published by a trade, an agent is probably the only way to go. That still leaves smaller publishers and academic presses open for aspiring fiction writers, though again, a query and proposal should always proceed submitting a full manuscript.

Agents work on commission, normally 15% of everything the author stands to receive, and their main function is to represent authors to publishers. Due to the huge volume of submissions that well-known agencies receive, it's not unreasonable for them to demand $100 as a way of forcing authors to think twice before sending in their work. However, you should research the agency on the Internet and in Literary Market Place (check your local library for a copy) to make sure that they make their living selling books to publishers and not selling dreams to authors. There are plenty of name agents who don't charge reading fees and who look down on those who do. In the end, it pays to concentrate on your query letter, and to read it once a day for a week to see if it really makes the best case it can for your book before sending it off.

Agency agreements can vary widely, from non-exclusive contracts that either party can terminate on short notice to exclusive representation with a long fade out period, so if the author terminates the agreement and sells the book three months later, the agent may still have the right to his or her cut. It's also normal for all author payments to be funneled through the agency, which ensures that they get their 15% without having to chase the author. If the agent is dishonest, incompetent or insolvent, the author may have to resort to the courts to try to recover money and get the publisher to change who the checks are made out to and where they get mailed. Agents may also charge their expenses to authors, anything from stamps and phone calls to travel and business luncheons, so make sure you aren't signing a blank check.

Perhaps the only way to make sure that you're getting a fair shake from an agent is to get a good book lawyer to review the agency agreement. If you aren't a member of a professional organization that offers free legal reviews, it's worth the money to hire a lawyer with experience in the field. Your local Bar association can give you a referral. In many instances, the member lawyer may give you 20 minutes or a half-hour of free time to see if you suit each other, and you'll get the agreement reviewed for free. Some lawyers also function as book agents, though that still leaves you with the problem of finding another lawyer to look at the agreement you have to sign with the agent/lawyer.

Some authors leave all of the contract negotiations to their agent, under the assumption that the agent has the author's best interests at heart. That seems intuitively correct, since the agent gets paid a percentage of what the author makes, but there's a catch. The vast majority of agents don't make their living off of a single author but through representing dozens or even hundreds of clients. The agents, therefore, have every reason to maintain the best relationships possible with acquisitions editors and publishers, to keep the door open for the next time they have a project to sell. That doesn't work in the author's best interest, and some writers have accused agents of selling them into poor contracts to score points with publishers. The best way to find a good agent is through referral from an author who has used that agent through several book deals and has been happy with the results.

If you can find a publisher on your own but you're worried, with good cause, about getting a fair contract, you should retain a lawyer. When you find a lawyer you're happy with and who you want to be available for consultation, you'll be asked for a retainer, a cash payment equal to a couple of hours of the lawyer's billing rate that is held in escrow. If there's something left over when the negotiations are finished, you can have the money returned, but it's probably better to keep the lawyer on retainer for future questions. Some authors will turn to agents for contract negotiation even if they've sold a book on their own, claiming that agents do the most book deals and know best. I know some authors who have taken this route, but I suspect their main motivation was to avoid the out-of-pocket expense for a good intellectual property lawyer with contract negotiation experience. Some of the choice will be dictated by your financial state, but keep in mind that the lawyer is a one-time expense, while the agent's hand stays in your pocket as long as the book sells and will probably stay in there for any future editions as well.

Publishing Contracts

The publishing industry has a bad reputation amongst the majority of writers, many of whom see publishers as little more than law firms with an editorial department in tow. Publishers reel in unwary authors with a carrot, the advance, then whack them with a stick, the contract. An acquisitions editor is an employee at the publisher whose job it is to sign authors to write books. Most new authors fail to retain legal counsel before signing their first contract, and actually depend on the acquisitions editor to tell them what's fair and normal for the publisher to request. This creates an excellent negotiating position for the publisher and a horrible one for the author. Unfortunately, publishers really take advantage.

Author advocacy organizations can be a good source for contract advice, but the catch is you usually have to be a published writer before you can join. There's nothing quite like the feeling of joining a prestigious author's guild after publishing a trade book, sending them the contract for your next edition for free legal review, and hearing something like, "Oh, you never should have signed the first contract. Now you're stuck with it forever."

Subsidy publisher contracts may outwardly resemble trade publisher contracts, but there's no reason you should be giving away any rights at all when you're paying them to publish the book. Don't fall for the line that the fee you're paying only offsets part of the production cost, blah, blah, blah. A good subsidy publisher will offer a short contract that describes the publisher's responsibilities, a royalty schedule, and how the author can (quickly) terminate the agreement. Some subsidy publishers hide their contract details until the last minute, hoping you'll sign simply because you've gone so far down the path. Don't even consider a subsidy publisher who doesn't have their author contract available on their website where you can read it before you contact them.

The contractual relationship between the author and the publisher is based on what's written in the signed contract, not on implicit understandings. Even experienced authors and agents sometime make the mistake of concentrating on the money and not paying enough attention to the clauses that protect the author's rights. All contract terms are negotiable, though acquisitions editors like to pretend they have a standard contract that all their authors are happy to sign. A brief summary of standard trade publisher contract terms follows, but it's by no means all-inclusive: I advise everyone who is looking at a contract signing to consult a lawyer.

Grant of Rights

Here the author grants the publisher the right to publish the work, as protected by copyright law. For most authors this means the exclusive worldwide rights, including all derivative works, etc. While it's not in the interests of the author to give up anything without negotiation, the publisher is frequently in a better position than the author to exploit these rights (such as publishing translations), which will result in further payments to the author. If the author believes the work is likely to become a smash TV hit or the next big Christmas toy, the derivative rights could be the plum of the contract.

Competing Works

Many nonfiction publishers try to get an author to commit to a non-compete clause. In a non-compete clause, the author agrees not to produce another work that competes with the title under contract without prior permission of the publisher. It's usually not in the interest of an author to write books that compete with each other, since this fractionates the market and may cause both books to fail. Experienced authors will not sign a contract with a non-compete clause, and publishers aren't going to promise not to publish books that compete directly with the author's, so it's just a bad deal. If the publisher insists on a non-compete from a new author, it should at least be narrowed to the point that the only way to violate it would be to write an essentially identical book. If you've signed a contract with a non-compete, it's worth talking to a lawyer to find out just how limited you really are.

Author's Warranty

The author is asked to guarantee that the work is actually theirs to sell, not plagiarized, stolen, or already sold to another publisher. This includes rights for any materials or illustrations in the book that the author didn't create. A paraphrase of the final line in this clause goes something like: "This warranty goes on forever and we'll dig you up to pay our legal fees if we get sued." This is really scary stuff because the author could get stuck paying NYC lawyer fees for a frivolous suit. While publishers will rightfully insist on an author's warranty, the language should limit the author's liability so the author doesn't get stuck paying the publisher's legal costs for something that isn't the author's fault. Keep any permissions you get from contributors in your long term files and keep your fingers crossed.

Manuscript Preparation

The deliverable of the contract is the manuscript, which is outlined here in size and content, including counts for the number of pages, words and illustrations. Acquisitions editors can be very casual about this description in order to maintain the maximum flexibility, even if the author has a pretty exact idea what the final numbers will be. There's no reason the editor shouldn't agree to describe the book as exactly what the author has agreed to write. The actual form of the manuscript is also detailed here, normally a Word file is required, though a couple printed copies and any artwork may also required. If the book will have an index, some reference to how that index will be prepared is often mentioned here or in a later paragraph. Authors shouldn't be asked to pay the expense of creating an index, but some contracts casually charge a couple thousand dollars against author royalties, or several dollars per book page. While the author should be willing to create an index if requested, paying the publisher to do it is ridiculous, and this language should be stricken from the contract.

Viability and Publication Delay

Publishers will also include language granting them the right to reject the manuscript the author presents, either requiring changes or canceling the contract. Determining the fitness of a manuscript for publication may sound like a subjective judgement, but a contract should contain some description of what makes a manuscript "fit for publication" to allow the author to contest the issue if the publisher cancels the book after the manuscript is submitted. Some books are years in the making, and the more time an author invests in a work the more important it is to nail down the conditions that must be met for publication. The author should also seek some language limiting the publisher's right to make changes beyond routine copy-editing without the author's approval. If the book is cancelled for any reason, the author should retain the advance money paid, and the full rights to the work should revert to the author for potential sale elsewhere.

Copyright

The publisher will often seek to register the copyright in place of the author. There may be some financial benefit to the publisher in owning the copyright if somebody actually infringes on it, since the proceeds of a lawsuit might then go to the publisher and not the author. However, the author has already assigned the rights to publish the book at the beginning of the contract, so even if the author retains the copyright, it doesn't mean the book remains the author's property. For what it's worth, the professional author's organization I belong to strongly recommends that authors retain their copyrights.

Proofing and Editing

The publisher will reserve the right to make revisions, which will ideally be subject to the author's approval. Whether or not that approval is required, the author must promptly review revisions for errors. Publishers also establish a level of changes that they will allow the author to make in the final stages of production, often 10% or 15% of the cost of preparing the proofs, above which the author will be charged against royalties. That may be fair if the author is trying to substantially rewrite the manuscript late in the production process. However, there should be no fee for correcting problems that are due to the publisher or their outsourced book designer introducing a large number of errors, whatever the cost. When an outsourced book designer ruined a book of mine such that every page had to be redone, the publisher "generously" agreed not to charge for the rework.

Publication

The primary thing separating a trade publisher from a subsidy press is that a trade publisher undertakes to pay the publication expenses of the book. The publisher will seek language that allows them to publish the book in the time that suits them, but authors should obtain some upper limit on this. It's entirely normal for publishers to miss their target dates by more than a month, in part due to a constant turnover of employees, but they should be willing to set a date at which the manuscript will revert to the author if they fail to publish. If the publisher wants a clause that would return any advances paid in this case, it should be dependent on the successful sale of the manuscript to another publisher.

Royalties

This is usually the longest section in the book contract, and describes the division of the money, provided the author hasn't written the book for a one-time payment in a work-for-hire arrangement. There's no real standard for domestic royalties, which is the most profitable segment of sales for most authors. It depends on the genre of the work and the publishing house. Ignoring super-star authors who write their own tickets, the best rate most writers can hope for is 15% of the cover price of trade hardcover books, with this percentage being achieved only after a certain number of copies have been sold. Many segments of the publishing industry have successfully changed that maximum to 15% of publisher net, which amounts to less than half the cover price. The lowest royalties I've heard of are less than 8% of net in genres like romance literature, where the publisher may even own the rights to the pen name under which the books are published.

It's common to set a number of steps with which the royalties escalate, setting a lower rate for the first 5,000 copies, a higher rate for the next 5,000, and only reaching the maximum rate after 10,000 or more copies have been sold. These break points may be one of the easier issues to negotiate. I've found it easier to move the break points, even eliminating the lowest category, than to increase the final royalty. Make sure you understand what books are actually being counted towards the royalty steps. In contracts I've signed, only the domestic full price sales have counted, which means that as much as half of my sales haven't counted toward increasing my royalty.

Advances

One thing that should be included in any trade contract is an advance against royalties. Advances are traditionally intended to support the author financially while they are in the process of writing the book. Advance payments may be split into multiple phases, with a payment for signing and further payments for reaching milestones in completing the contract requirements. Some publishers may spread partial payments over the whole production process, even all the way up to the publication date. Many publishers pay their bills so slowly that an author in a hurry may submit the final manuscript before receiving the signing payment. If the publisher cancels the contract at this point, it may prove difficult or impossible for the author to obtain any advance money, as possession is nine-tenths of the law. The lowest advance I've been offered by a trade publisher is $2,000 (split over four payments), the highest was $13,000.

Publishers can actually be very flexible on advances, which they use to try to lure authors into signing bad contracts. Since so many writers live a hand-to-mouth existence, the promise of an extra few thousand dollars up-front may lure them into signing a contract with a lower royalty rate or longer escalation schedule. It's always a gamble, and many trade authors never see any ongoing royalties because their books never sell enough copies to pay back the advance. Some authors and agents even feel that if the book does pay back the advance, it just means that they failed to negotiate a high enough advance to start with. I'm always optimistic that my books will sell, so I prefer a higher royalty to a larger advance, but if I thought I could get $100,000, I might sing a different tune.

Try not to sign any contracts with cross-accounting schemes, where payments due on one title may be charged against debits from another of your titles by the same publisher. Authors are under no legal or moral obligation to make sure a publisher never loses money on a book, it's part of the risk they undertake in claiming the lion's share of the income. If you have signed a cross-accounting clause in a contract with a publisher and they want another book from you, you can probably get them to leave it out of the new contract and modify the original contract so that the clause no longer applies. Otherwise, take the new title to another publisher. A cross-accounting clause shouldn't be viewed as a deal-breaker for a first book, since it has no impact unless you go on to write more books for the same publisher or the book goes into edition.

Foreign Sales

Publishers will always establish a different royalty schedule for foreign sales. The rate may be a little lower than the domestic royalty rate, but it shouldn't be a mere fraction. Publishers have been successfully sued for selling their own books to foreign subsidiaries at drastically reduced prices in order to reduce author royalties. It's best for the author to have foreign royalties based on the cover price, since overseas net is so easy to manipulate.

Deep Discounts and Book Clubs

Publishers sell books into different outlets at different prices, and when they earn less they like to pay the author less. There's no reason the author should agree to such an arrangement, but it's become quite standard, and the best most authors can hope for is that both parties share the pain equally. It's in the interest of the author to limit special pricing as much as possible, since the royalty will be greatly reduced while the special sales may cannibalize the author's domestic sales. Authors should pay special attention to deep discount clauses, which allow publishers to sharply reduce, even halve author royalties, if the sale price falls below a set percentage of the cover. This creates a situation where it's actually more profitable for the publisher to sell books at the deep discount than just above it, since the reduction in the author's royalty more than offsets the amount of the reduction in the selling price.

Sale of Rights

Publishers who acquire the exclusive international rights for a book will set a royalty schedule for when those rights are sold to third parties or their own overseas subsidiaries. Splits of 50/50 on net receipts are common, though some publishers try to get authors to agree to base the split on the domestic royalty schedule, amounting to a quarter or a fifth of the amount a 50/50 split on publisher net would generate. Foreign rights are sold so cheaply for most books, sometimes for as low as a few hundred dollars, that anything less than a 50/50 split barely produces pocket change for an author. Translation rights for some of my own trade published computer books have been: $1,300 for a Chinese translation, $595 for Arabic, $2000 for Russian, $450 for Polish.

Payments

The contract establishes a schedule for when the accounting is done and payments are made. Quarterly royalty payments are normal, though they will lag the actual sales period by a month or two. Some publishers still push semi-annual payments, with royalties for the January 1st through June 30th period being due before September 30th. Some publishers may agree to pay within 30 days of the end of the accounting period. Authors should try to have a clause inserted that allows them to have an independent auditor check the publisher's accounts.

Reserve Against Returns

Publishers usually insist on a clause allowing them to establish "a reasonable reserve against returns." The intention of the clause is to protect the publisher against paying the author for books that are sitting on store shelves but may eventually be returned to the publisher. It's best to have this "reasonable reserve" spelled out, both in terms of the percentage of total sales to be held in reserve and the length of time for which the publisher can hold the money.

A 20% or less reserve may be viewed as reasonable, though some publishers attempt to hold out for much higher amounts. The reserve retention period will likely be a year or longer, though two years is probably the longest period that can be justified by market economics. The main risk for the author is that the publisher goes out of business and any sums owed the author are unrecoverable.

Author's Copies

The author can expect a dozen or more free copies of the book to give to friends and family. Publishers should always be happy to provide free review copies of books and may offer to take care of the shipping and handling. There is often the option for the author to buy more copies at a discount, though these books won't be counted towards the author's royalties and there may be restrictions on selling them.

Revised Editions

Publishers will insist on the right to publish revised editions of the work. The author should insist on the right to do those editions. The publisher will want the right to get another writer if the original author is unavailable to do a new edition on a reasonable time schedule after the publisher requests it. However, the original author or his heirs should continue to receive royalties. These royalties will be at a reduced rate, and the author should try to negotiate that the reduction be based on the extent of the revisions. The author may also seek to negotiate the right not to have later editions published under the author's name if the author doesn't participate. An open-ended clause that would allow the publisher to spend profligately on producing a new edition and debit the amount from the author's royalties should be avoided if at all possible.

Out of Print

A book is only out of print when the publisher declares it so and updates the ISBN record to reflect this fact. It may also be considered out of print for the purpose of reversion of rights to the author if it is no longer available from the publisher in any edition. The author may have to go through a set procedure, such as requesting in writing that the book be reprinted and waiting a pre-defined time period, but afterwards the rights should revert to the author. One of the problems with print-on-demand is it allows publishers to keep books in print indefinitely when availability is the only test. The author should seek to clarify this contract language as much as possible, setting a minimum number of books sold or moneys earned in consecutive royalty periods, after which the book will be deemed out of print.

Book Packagers and Consultants

Traditional book packagers are industry professionals who take an author's manuscript, put it together with a design and a marketing plan, then sell the whole package to a trade publisher. Some agents double as book packagers and vice-versa, since the two functions are closely related. In recent years, people acting as publishing consultants are also calling themselves book packagers, a phenomena rising out of the massive increase in self-publishing combined with the self-promotional possibilities for consultants on the Internet. These new style book packagers charge authors to prepare a manuscript for publication and to consult on the marketing plan, sometimes acting as publicists as well. It's closely akin to subsidy publishing, in that the author pays all the fees up front, and some of these book packagers function as subsidy presses as well.

There's a good reason to be suspicious of book packagers and consultants who are authors and publishers themselves, but who have to sell their expert services to make ends meet. They may be highly ethical and their services may look like inexpensive insurance to authors or publishers who are just starting out, but I'd be skeptical of any book packager who doesn't have a long list of prior clients whom you can contact. Some book packagers offer access to distribution as part of their service and if they can get you a better distribution deal than you can find for yourself, there's some value there. Consultants, on the other hand, are an expensive and often unnecessary expense in any business, and publishing is no exception. Be especially wary of Internet discussion list participants who are always making scary posts about how complicated and difficult every facet of publishing is and simultaneously advertise their own services in their signature.

Finding a Publisher in the Internet Age

Imagine sending a query letter offering an unfinished manuscript to eight publishers and getting back four positive responses within the week. How about having the managing editor of a major imprint contact you out of the blue asking if you have a publisher for your work? These may sound like scenarios from an advertisement in a writer's magazine intended to separate you from your money, but they actually happened for this author, thanks to a personal website. The vast majority of writers today have exchanged their typewriters for personal computers, but their sole focus remains the double-spaced manuscript that gets sent off to New York City with a SASE. That's a shame because by simply skipping down an extra item in the **File** menu of your word processor, you can save that document as HTML, a form ready for instant publication on the Internet.

"Why should I give my work away for free?" you argue, "What if somebody steals it?" If you're an unpublished writer, getting people to read your work and respond to it is the primary challenge. After all, you need to convince the editors or agents you contact that you really know your market, but how can you actually do that if your market has never heard of you? Whether you are writing plumbing books or poetry, there is an audience for your work on the Internet, and if you can fix their leaky hearts, some of them will send e-mail to let you know how much they appreciate you. By the way, a copyright is a copyright, so if somebody does plagiarize your work, take it as a compliment and threaten to sue.

Testimonial e-mails from visitors to your site can carry real weight with an acquisitions editor. In fact, the publisher used excerpts from nine such letters as a marketing tool on the back cover of my first published book, "The Hand-Me-Down PC." Feedback from web surfers is valuable for another reason; this audience isn't tied to you by friendship or by blood. Any criticism is useful because these people ARE your market, and compliments from Mom are rarely as uplifting as praise from complete strangers. Traffic on your site can be used as a form of proof that you do have an audience, and even more importantly for smaller publishers, that you know how to promote yourself.

There is one exercise in market research that anyone who wants to be published must undertake. Put yourself in the shoes of your target audience and search the web for the sort of work you hope to publish. You'll gain valuable insight into the competition, an important part of any sales pitch to publishers. You may be astounded by the number of sites that already offer something similar to what you were planning to pioneer, but don't be discouraged. In publishing, the bigger the existing market, the more willing a publisher is to produce another title for it. Conversely, if you can't find anything on the web similar to your work, you could be in trouble. The worst thing you can do when pitching a title to a publisher is to brag about how unique your work is. Nobody in the real business world wants to touch anything that's unique. Just like Hollywood keeps producing sequels, serious business people are looking for proven moneymaking ideas, not "unique" opportunities.

Maybe you secretly hate your computer, though you avoid thinking about it while you're working for fear it will read your mind and trash your documents. There will always be room for a small number of eccentrics whose eccentricities are part and parcel of their attraction, but it's a tough role to break in with. The Internet is the future, and a web strategy will be an integral part of any query letter in the coming years. The best way to learn about the web and its potential is to get online and experiment with it. Even if you never build your own website, you're going to need to understand how the publishing industry uses this tool. If you visit trade publisher websites, you'll be surprised to see how many acquisitions editors have their e-mail address posted online. Sending an old-fashioned query letter with an SASE in the mail to an editor who posts his or her e-mail address online isn't just a waste of two stamps, it increases the risk that the query letter will never even get read.

Trade Publishing

Major trade publishers, who produce the majority of the books found on bookstore shelves, have been following the same basic model since the Great Depression of the 1930's. In order for these publishers to stay in business during the Depression, they needed to keep the bookstores open and selling their books. Since the bookstores didn't have the resources to pay for enough books to stock a store, the publishers made all books returnable for credit, and didn't push the bookstores to pay their bills. In other words, bookselling became a consignment business. Even those books that the retailers paid for could be returned years later for full credit against the bills they currently owed the publisher or distributor. Some publishers stop accepting returns a set number of months after a title is declared "out-of-print," others accept returns without any time limit. The three factors that currently define trade publishing are: large print runs on offset presses, trade discounts to distributors (often 55% or more off the cover price), and generous returns policies.

Distribution, Discounts and Returns

Not surprisingly, returns are a millstone around the neck of traditional publishers, with some major trades experiencing return rates over 30% in bad years. Imagine printing a large run of books, shipping all your stock to retailers, printing another run, only to have the books from the original print run start coming back. Now you've nowhere to put the books from the old print run, and the profits you thought you were earning on their sales evaporate. Even worse, if the original print run didn't sell, the odds aren't good that any of the books now in stock will ever be sold. One way publishers can limit the number of returns is to sell books at a deep discount (usually more than 60% off the cover) on a non-returnable basis, but this accounts for a relatively small fraction of trade sales. Returns, particularly those of paperback books, often arrive back at the publisher in a condition that prevents their being sold as new, even if demand for the title exists.

There are several tiers of distributors and wholesalers, and many people in the book business like to argue about their definitions. Some distributors require publishers to sign exclusive contracts to use them for distribution of their titles, and these master distributors will ship books to other distributors and wholesalers, in addition to direct bookstore sales. Niche distributors may only accept publishers they feel they can succeed with, and invest money and time marketing their "list" to bookstores. Wholesalers simply fill the warehousing and shipping function for publishers who do all of their own marketing but who don't want to be involved in order fulfillment. Smaller chain and independent bookstores rely heavily on book distributors and wholesalers to fill orders and handle centralized returns. Major bookstore chains such as Barnes&Noble and Borders have their own warehouse and distribution systems, allowing them to deal directly with a large number of publishers whose sales volume justifies the relationship.

The biggest American book distributor is the Ingram Book Company, and they reach over 90% of the book retailers in the U.S. While Ingram has some special programs for small publishers with sufficient sales, they refer most small publishers to other distributors who have an Ingram relationship. Since Ingram makes available hundreds of thousand of titles, they don't have a sales force promoting a list of books to retailers in the same sense that some distributors do, and many people consider Ingram to be a wholesaler. Ingram "buys" books at a variety of discounts, depending on the arrangement they have with the publisher. Some academic publishers manage to sell their books to Ingram at the list price, but Ingram will "up-price" these to provide enough profit to make doing business feasible. Small publishers who qualify to work directly with Ingram are usually asked for a 55% or 60% discount. Baker&Taylor is the second largest distributor in the U.S.; they specialize in library and education sales. Baker&Taylor will purchase books from publishers on a short discount, non-returnable basis, but only for existing orders. Most other distributors and wholesalers demand discounts of 60% to 70% from publishers, and often set minimum quantities for stocking and charge a warehousing fee for unsold books (until they return them).

Frontlist and Backlist

Trade publishers focus all their energy and marketing dollars on their new titles, know as "frontlist." These are the titles their sales force will promote to book buyers at shows, through catalog mailings and through trade advertising, usually before the titles are actually published. The goal of frontlist advertising is to persuade bookstores and distributors to pre-order these titles in quantity, to help fix the size of the print run and to make sure the books will be available on shelves for any publicity the book launch generates. Sometimes publishers will announce a large print run in advance of the sales blitz to convince the chain buyers they are confident the book will be a bestseller. Small publishers attempt to do the same on a much more limited scale, with the ultimate goal being to get multiple copies of the titles onto the chain shelves where they'll have the greatest chance of a major success.

When you hear authors or other book industry professionals discussing a five week window for a book to generate demand, they're talking about a period right around the release date when the publisher is willing to invest in promotion. For most titles, this begins a few weeks before the release and extends a couple weeks after. It's a reality of trade publishing that, with multiple titles released every week, the sales force focuses on the newest books and the potential blockbusters, whose famous authors received a large advance which the publisher needs to recoup. Another figure you'll hear discussed is the four months a new title has to prove itself. This is about how long most bookstores will give a new title to start selling. With all the computerization in the chains and the availability of industry wide sales numbers from Nielsen's BookScan, it doesn't take long to determine whether or not a new title is earning its place on the shelves.

Backlist titles are books that remain in print for years and continue to sell at a steady rate. Some backlist titles, classic novels for example, out-sell most frontlist titles year after year. Most trade publishers derive a significant portion of their income from backlist titles; for some, it's the backlist that earns the majority of the profits and supports the frontlist. A strong backlist is the backbone of a successful publishing house, whether large or small, and when publishers acquire each other it's usually to get their hands on the backlist. Some people differentiate between frontlist and backlist by the allocation of advertising dollars. Any book that isn't being actively marketed can be lumped into the backlist category, regardless of the publication date.

Imprints and Branding

Most major trade publishers use imprints as a way to differentiate between the genres they publish and to lessen the "mega-corporation" feel for book buyers. Imprints at large publishers are frequently characterized by the backlist and by the theme of smaller publishers they've acquired. Most imprints are a soft form of branding, based on long term reputation and consistency rather than aggressive marketing. Publishers sometimes redistribute books within their imprints for internal reasons, so authors may find a new edition of their book has a different publisher name on the cover, though the royalty check still comes from the parent company.

The power of branding is an acknowledged fact in the modern publishing business, so anytime a publisher can establish a series of books with name recognition, they ride it for all it's worth. The easiest way to build a brand is around an existing bestseller. Only large publishers have the deep pockets and staying power to try to build a brand by introducing a dozen or more newly branded titles simultaneously. At first glance, branding may look like a very efficient publishing process because of the savings on cover art and book design, which is applied to all the books in the brand. However, introducing a whole stable of unproven titles in a short time period is a huge risk, since it's quite possible that none of them will sell.

Nonfiction brands are usually replete with common features known as "elements" to help reinforce the brand. These may be little reminders, cute warnings, or any other number of features peripheral to the actual writing which serve to establish a common identity for the books. Branded nonfiction titles are frequently proposed and produced by in-house editors in support of the brand concept. These are often reference works, and are often written by work-for-hire authors, whether named or anonymous, who receive no royalties for the book. The unrelenting pressure for new titles plus the pressure to squeeze the last drop out of an investment in branding combine to eventually dilute most brands to the point of abandonment.

Publication Process

There's no set formula for how trade publishers actually go about producing the titles they publish, but the focus for the last couple of decades has been on cost control through outsourcing. Some publishing houses consist of little more than acquisitions editors, salespeople, accountants, lawyers and management. Though that might sound like an exaggeration, outsourcing every phase of book production from editing and proofreading to cover design and interior layout is increasingly common, and no self-respecting publisher would actually own a printing press.

Some publishing houses allow authors to deliver manuscripts in one installment, although the editor may keep tabs on the work in progress. Many nonfiction books are submitted piecemeal, from as little as a chapter at a time, to three or four major deliverable dates. The production editor for the book (the individual who shepherds it through the publication process) may be the same as the acquisitions editor, it varies by publisher. The one thing you can be relatively sure of is that mistakes will occur. Production editors are notoriously over tasked, working on anywhere from a dozen to two dozen books at a time. This level of multi-tasking is horrendously inefficient, since the humans end up spending all their time swapping between tasks. Just imagine maintaining a dozen threads of correspondence with individual sets of authors, copy editors, technical editors, proofreaders, cover artists, book designers, marketing staff, etc. A typical editor at a trade publisher can easily receive over 100 non-spam e-mails a day, so if you find yourself in a correspondence with one, keep it short and get the main idea into the first sentence. Superstar authors and books receive better treatment, since the publisher can justify "under utilizing" the editor(s) involved based on the expected reward. In most cases, the responsibility for producing a quality book falls squarely on the author's shoulders, and it can require a fighting spirit to get even the most jarring mistakes corrected once the production is put on a schedule.

Remainders and Internet Booksellers

Publishers typically remainder books that are taking up warehouse space with no apparent future, selling them in bulk for pennies on the dollar. Some publishers begin remaindering books as soon as the first wave of returns comes in from bookstores, which can happen within a few months of publication. Books can also find their way into the remainder market from bookstores or distributors who purchased them outright, don't want to be bothered with returning them to the publisher, or are authorized by the publisher to act as a middleman to save on shipping and handling. The publisher may be lucky to recoup the printing cost on remaindered books, though it helps to close the bookkeeping inventory loop for the IRS. The only other option for a publisher with a large number of unsold books is to recycle them as paper pulp. The traditional marketplaces for remaindered books in pre-Internet days were specialty mail order houses, traveling remainder shows, or a special remainder tables in regular bookstores. These sales didn't hurt authors because customers who were actually looking for a book were likely to order it at the retail price through a bookstore, not wait indefinitely in hopes of stumbling across it as a remainder.

The Internet has irrevocably changed the economics of remaindering. Where the remaindering process was once a convenient way of reducing handling costs on returns, even for titles that were strong sellers, it's turned into a tax on both publishers and authors. Remaindered books now compete directly with the new copies on Internet bookseller sites. Shoppers at Amazon.com often find new books being sold by Amazon Marketplace sellers for well under half the cover price with a small note to the effect of "may have remainder mark." This understandably drives authors nuts, since they may earn no royalty on the sale. The world of online bookselling allows books from any and all sources to sit next to each other on the same virtual shelf and compete on price and price alone. Publishers have been very slow to realize that the Internet has changed their traditional business model. The majority of them still don't get it, and it may take a new generation of management before they come to their senses.

Editions and Oversaturation

A book that is changed or updated in a substantial way and assigned a new ISBN is termed a new edition. A new edition of a novel may arise from something as basic as a change in the physical book design, such as a larger font or a different binding, or from something more substantial, such as the addition of a critical introduction and notes, or illustrations. Successful nonfiction books usually appear in a new edition with updated material. Updates may have no real impact on the narrative thread, such as the addition of more contemporary example problems in a textbook, or they may consist primarily of adding new chapters, creating an ever heavier and more expensive reference. Nonfiction professional books that go into edition are similar to bestselling novels on a backlist, except the professional books need to go through the revision process on a regular basis to maintain their sales. Nonfiction books in edition often lose their market share, despite having a strong head start, if minimal revisions are made just for the sake of refreshing the copyright date and slapping a new edition number on the cover.

In the area of nonfiction publishing, which accounts for the vast majority of trade titles published every year, any title going into edition will attract the attention of other publishers and authors and competing titles will certainly follow. Publishers looking to wring every possible sale out of a niche market are often the first to produce titles that compete with a successful book of their own, though they will try to pass it off as synergy rather than competition. Finding out just how many different titles a niche market can support is an ongoing experiment that always results in failure for a large number of new entrants, and may actually result in an overall loss of sales for the niche if the publisher dilutes the market too far. The market can become so fractionated that none of the individual titles from the original publisher sell enough copies to justify their precious spot on bookstore shelves. This allows a new publisher with a reasonable title and more focused marketing approach to get multiple copies onto bookstore shelves and take over the niche.

Print-on-Demand

The least imaginative use of print-on-demand is to take the traditional trade publishing model and to replace the offset press with POD. The primary tradeoffs are a higher unit cost and lower print quality in return for lower capital and overhead costs and the elimination of inventory. Not surprisingly, this is how most trade publishers and academic presses have applied the new technology to their business models, relegating it to a fulfillment role for slower selling backlist titles. It would be difficult to argue for the major trades to switch to POD, due to the simple economics of the huge print-runs required for the frontlist model. Unlike the big trades, small publishers, however ambitious they may be, have to deal with the reality of limited financing and market muscle. This is especially true for new imprints and self-publishers, from whom the traditional approach demands a major financial gamble with little realistic hope of earning a living from the results.

In its most basic sense, POD is a new printing technology that allows a single copy of a book to be printed from a stored computer file. The price for a single unit is competitive with the price a traditional offset printer charges per unit for a short-run (an order of a few hundred books), if the total page count isn't too high. Just about all of the major publishers, both trade and academic, are already using POD to keep older titles in print or to publish niche books that would otherwise be economically unfeasible. It's quite likely you've already purchased or read a POD book without even knowing it.

This book is printed by Lightning Source, the largest print-on-demand printer in America. Lightning Source is owned by Ingram Industries Inc, making it a sister company to Ingram Book Company, the largest book distributor in the country. Publishers using Lightning Source gain hands-off access to Ingram distribution. Hopefully, this book is selling sufficiently well that it's being printed in quantities of 20 or 50 copies at a time to meet demand. However, as long as we pay the $12/year fee to keep the electronic file in the Lightning Source library, the book will remain in print and available within a few days to the majority of U.S. and U.K. buyers, even if it is only selling one copy a year.

POD is as much a departure from traditional publishing as e-mail is from surface mail. E-mail carries with it the curse of spam, since the e-mail costs are so low that spammers can send out millions of messages at a time. Surface mail is also plagued by junk mail but the cost of the mailings pretty much ensures that you won't receive hundreds of pieces a day. Similarly, POD has lowered the capital investment required for book production to almost zero, bringing with it a flood of books from subsidy presses. Subsidy presses, which take a fee from authors to publish their books, now flood the book market with tens of thousands of titles a year, the vast majority of which will never sell a dozen copies. POD has been a boon for authors who choose to publish through a subsidy press because the old offset based subsidy presses charged thousands or tens of thousands of dollars, rather than hundreds of dollars, to get an aspiring author into print. Some people in the publishing industry sneer at these "junk books," and when they claim that POD books aren't accepted or successful in the marketplace, they're talking about subsidy press books, not the actual printing technology.

A Year in the Life of a POD Title

People who have worked in the publishing industry in any capacity are often dubious of the claims made for the print-on-demand publishing model, because it violates the "rules" of publishing as they know them. Our best answer to the critics is to start off with a case study of a year in the life of an actual POD book, published by the author through Lightning Source, including the actual sales, profits, and trends. It's important to get an overview of the whole process and costs at the outset. If you have trouble following the discussion the first time through, just keep an eye on the dollars.

"Start Your Own Computer Business" was published by Foner Books in December 2002. The book is a 6" x 9" paperback at 168 pages, and Lightning Source charges Foner Books $3.09 for each copy printed for distribution. The first thing that will occur to anybody who has been involved in traditional publishing is that the same book could be printed on an offset press for around $1.00 each in large quantity. Here's where the POD and traditional publishing models diverge. There never are "large quantities" involved with POD, no tons of books to warehouse or thousands of dollars to tie up in inventory. Even more important for a small publisher using Lighting Source, there's no shipping cost for books sold into distribution.

Publishers sell books to distributors and bookstores at a discount off the cover price, enabling the final retail outlet and any middlemen to make a profit. The normal discount rate that distributors require from publishers, the percentage off the cover price the publisher gives the distributor for a book that they resell to a retail outlet, is 55% or more. Small offset publishers who qualify for Ingram distribution may be charged 60%, and other distributors can charge 70% or more of the cover price to stock and distribute your books. In other words, the only time a publisher is ever paid the cover price on their books is if they sell them directly to the customer, usually by mail order.

Ingram will carry Lightning Source POD books on a "short-discount" basis, a discount less than 55%. Foner Books assigned a 35% discount on the $14.95 cover price of "Start Your Own Computer Business" so the book is sold by Lightning Source to Ingram, Amazon, and other wholesale customers, for $9.72. Here's where the math really departs from the traditional publishing model: $9.72 - $3.09 (the printing fee) leaves the publisher (Foner Books) with $6.63, which happens to be 44% of the cover price. This price was chosen to correspond with the average net for a trade publisher before expenses such as book development, author royalties, etc. This 44% of the cover is entirely hands-off, with no inventory or storage costs, no shipping and handling, and virtually no returns since the book is only printed in accordance with demand.

Foner Books also chose to sell books direct from our website at a 20% discount. The delivered cost for short run of 25 books is $93.66 or $3.74 each. Our 20% off mail order price of $11.95 leaves a profit of $8.21 per book, and customers pay a $2.25 shipping and handling fee which covers the average cost of a mailer and postage. Direct mail order sales during 2003 earned 55% of the cover price, while maintaining an average inventory of less than 25 books! Many authors can compare this to the 4 % to 7.5% of the cover price they earn in royalties on domestic, full price sales of paperback books. An author willing to gamble on this self-publishing model can make ten times as much per book sold as compared with royalty income from a major trade house. With many books generating more than a tenth of their sales through Amazon alone, where trade publisher muscle carries little or no weight, one wonders what the trade publishers have to offer authors whose books aren't destined to become fiction bestsellers.

Compare these numbers to the traditional offset printing model. Printing the same book on offset, we would have to increase the page count to 176 (a multiple of 16 pages) for 8-up printing. The following pricing was obtained online at the print broker Rjcom.com, and doesn't include shipping or fees:

Quantity	200	500	1000	2000	5000	10000
Price	$5.26	$4.50	$2.60	$1.63	$1.04	$0.83

It takes a run of about 750 copies to get the offset printing cost per book down to the POD cost, and we'd still have to pay for delivery and storage. If the only sales channel was direct mail order, we'd be at break even with the POD model, but how about distribution, which generated over 80% of the sales for the case study title in 2003? Ingram might have agreed to carry the book in their small publisher program for a 60% discount, plus shipping costs. Amazon, through their Advantage program, would carry the book for a 55% discount, plus a small yearly fee and recurring shipping and handling costs. At 55% of the $14.95 cover price, Foner Books would have netted $6.72 per book, but would have been required to pay for shipping. Even if we had gambled on printing 10,000 books to bring the cost per book down to $0.83, the maximum profit would have been $5.89 per book, minus returns, warehousing, shipping, packing materials, and the cost of money. The hands-off $6.63 per book earned from Lightning Source is actually more than we would have earned by gambling on a huge offset print run, thanks to the short discount that's otherwise unavailable to most small publishers.

2003 Sales Progression by Outlet

2003 Sales	U.S. L.S.	Ingram[1]	U.K. L.S.	Mail Order	Total
January	63	23		12	75
February	46	34		10	56
March	81	53		18	99
April	55	45		29	84
May	87	49		25	112
June	131	69	3	18	152
July	106	59	3	32	141
August	112	49	8	21	141
September	213	101	3	41	257
October	82	96	6	24	112
November	214	75	2	7	223
December	147	131	14	10	171
2003 Total	1337	789	39	247	1623

[1] Ingram sales are included in U.S. Lightning Source Total

January – The book officially became available in December of 2002, but a couple dozen orders placed through Ingram and Amazon during the holiday rush weren't printed and shipped until January. Lightning Source tripled their printing capacity during 2003, and no serious delays were apparent during the 2003 holiday season. January sales were helped by the release of a book excerpt to a number of Internet newsletters.

February – In addition to being a short month, February was marked by higher web traffic with a lower sales to visitors ratio, or sell-through. This was due to experimenting with a subtle "soft sell" approach on the website that didn't work very well. Foner Books signed up with Ingram's iPage service, allowing us to monitor Ingram stocking, store demand and sales.

March – Foner Books signed up with PayPal to accept credit card and PayPal cash account payments for the book. Previously, we had sold mail order only by check or through Amazon Marketplace. Web traffic in March reached double the level it had been at the start of the year, thanks to the addition of new content to the site. March also brought the first of many requests from entrepreneurial types who wanted to buy the book in quantity at a deep discount for resale at a profit, a request we politely rejected.

April – Poor availability at Amazon put a dent in April sales, though direct sales through the website rose sharply to absorb some of the loss. The estimated shipping time from Amazon during this period frequently rose to **1 - 2 weeks** rather than **24 Hours** or **2 to 3 days**, a real turn-off for customers. The slow Amazon ship time probably resulted from their ramping up their order quantity more slowly than the increase in demand.

May – The first 100 copy month for our new title, sales were driven primarily by improving the book's Amazon standing through changing the subtitle and to increased website traffic. Originally, the book's full title was "Start Your Own Computer Business: The Unembellished Guide," but in April, we changed the subtitle to "Building a Successful PC Repair and Service Business by Supporting Customers and Managing Money." The change took several weeks to appear in the online catalogs. It was entered at BowkerLink and sent directly to Lightning Source, appearing everywhere by May.

June – Thanks to steadily increasing web traffic and building momentum, the title earned a spot in the top 10,000 books at Amazon, a level often used by trade publishers to determine a book's commercial viability. Between the strong sales and the subtitle changes, the book began placing at the top of Amazon searches for key phrases like "Computer Business" and "PC Business." Foner Books signs up for Lightning Source U.K. distribution after an e-mail request from a potential customer.

July – The relative success of the title leads to a Catch-22 where it's frequently out of stock at both Ingram and Amazon. Mail order sales hit a new high picking up some of the slack, but it's obvious that sales are being lost. Two Ingram warehouses order and stock Lighting Source books, and the book is out of stock at one or the other on 31 out of a possible 62 days, or 50% of the time.

August – Ingram and Amazon stocking problems continue, with the book out of stock at one or both warehouses a total of 34 out of 62 possible days. Web traffic is down at a time of family vacation and back-to-school preparations. Ingram sales slump to the lowest level in months.

September – Ingram stocking improves somewhat, missing 20 days out of a possible 60. Strong sales convince the Ingram buyer to order 80 books in one shot near the end of the month, overriding the automated water torture method of ordering five or six books at a time. Mail order sales hit a record high at the same time with the back-to-school increase in web traffic.

October – The book is in stock at Ingram all but five days out of a possible 62, and is never out at both warehouses on the same day. Lightning Source sales for the month are artificially low, since Ingram ordered enough stock in September to last most of the month. Mail order slumps because both Ingram and Amazon have the book in stock almost every day.

November – In order to encourage Ingram and Amazon to continue ordering the book in quantity, we instruct Lightning Source to change the returns policy from "No Returns" to "Returnable." Foner Books takes a vacation and shuts down our mail order operation for two weeks. Mail order continues to slow as customers are able to obtain the book elsewhere and become leery of possible holiday shipping delays.

December – Sales continue steadily, though the LSI numbers are distorted by another big Ingram stocking order in mid-November. The Amazon sales rank of the book drops into the high nine-thousand range, as gift books dominate December online sales. This is the lowest mail order month since February, as customers avoid the holiday mail crunch. Ingram sales hit record high, thanks to good stocking and customers' preference to order books through stores during the holiday season.

Year in Summary – Foner Books netted a little over $11,000 in profit during 2003 on sales of 1623 copies of "Start Your Own Computer Business." There were no returns reported through Lightning Source, and only two books shipped by direct mail "went missing." The book was designed from the outset for POD publication since the niche subject and low page count (168 pages) would have rendered it a poor candidate for bookstore sales. Sales momentum built throughout the year, with occasional glitches due primarily to availability issues and website traffic patterns. Sales continued to accelerate in the first quarter of 2004, proving that the demand in late 2003 was due to website traffic and word-of-mouth rather than holiday gift giving.

POD Myths

Myth #1 – The most prevalent myth about POD is that books published with on-demand technology are unwelcome in bookstores and libraries. Nothing could be further from the truth. In fact, the world's major academic presses are some of the heaviest users of POD. The factors that keep any new book from gaining a place on bookstore shelves are: lack of marketing, lack of demand, the publisher's refusal to accept returns, the publisher's refusal to grant the trade discount, or an unprofessional appearance.

Myth #2 – The second widely believed myth about POD books is that they are amateur productions. The technology used to print a book has no bearing on the production values, which result from a combination of writing, editing, proofreading and design. The quality of the paper stock and cover printing for POD books varies with the provider, just as it does with offset printed books.

Myth #3 – The third myth says that a publisher would choose POD only if they planned to print less than a hundred books a year. As we showed in our case study, POD can actually be cheaper for printing books in quantities up to 500 or more copies at a time, and allows an order turn-around time of days rather than weeks. A book that only sells 100 copies a year is not a compelling commercial product for any publisher, unless the cover price is astronomically high.

Myth #4 – Print-on-demand publishing equals vanity publishing. The truth is that practically all the major trade publishers in the country utilize POD for some portion of their backlist. This myth is probably the most damaging to POD as a branding expression, since it has become associated with the subsidy press business in the minds of most people working in the book industry. However, there's no reason for a customer to care about the technology used to create a book, unless the publisher wants to make the argument that POD technology is "tree friendly."

POD Technology

Print-on-demand uses the same toner based, digital printing technology as a laser printer. Some ambitious self-publishers, who aren't worried about distribution for niche titles they promote through professional activities, actually buy production quality laser printers and print and bind their own books one at a time. Paperback covers and dust jackets for case bindings are printed on color lasers using special paper stock. The paper stocks available for the cover, in addition to the binding type, are not universally available for all book sizes, so clarify the options with the printer before designing the book. The laser printers used for POD are truly industrial strength, pumping out multiple pages per second.

The miracle of print-on-demand technology is not the printing process itself, which is actually the weak link from the standpoint of most publishers, but the digital library behind it. Lightning Source already has over 125,000 books in their digital library, any one of which is typically printed and shipped within 48 hours of an order being placed. That library is growing at a rate of approximately 1,000 books a week. Printing books from digital files, rather than from the relatively expensive plates used in offset printing, means that corrections can be made at almost no expense, and with no pre-correction stock left to worry about. The hero of the digital library story is Portable Document Format (PDF) created by Adobe and used globally in conjunction with their free Acrobat reader. Most publishers choose to use the full version of Acrobat to prepare their titles for digital publication, although there are capable third party software products that also do the job.

POD Economics with Lightning Source

Printing costs on POD books published through Lightning Source have very straightforward economics. There's a small annual charge for maintaining a book in their digital library, after an up-front fee per title based on the page count. The numbers below reflect the costs for our case study book, but these are obviously subject to change at the discretion of Lightning Source.

Digital file submission and proof copy costs:

Cover - $50
Interior - 168 pages @ $0.15 / page = $25.20
Proof - $30 (includes delivery to publisher)
Total Setup cost - $105.20

Lightning Source has two different printing charges for books, one for books they sell into distribution for the publisher (wholesale orders) and a slightly higher charge for publisher direct orders. For books sold into distribution, Lightning Source charges Foner Books:

Cover - $0.90
Interior - 168 pages @$0.013 / page = $2.19
Total per book = $3.09

For books we order directly for resale through our own channels, including shipping and handling for the quantity 25 we typically order:

Cover $0.90
Interior - 168 pages @ $0.015 / page = $2.52
Total = $3.82 /book (delivered)

Lightning Source allows the publisher to assign a discount of anywhere between 20% to 55% to a title for sale into distribution. In my experience, if a publisher assigns a discount of less than 25%, the book will be up-priced (restickered at a higher price) by distributors and Amazon, but this depends on their policies, not Lightning Source. With our cover price of $14.95, we chose a discount of 35% to encourage bookstores to order to meet demand (they can make a profit) but to discourage them from ordering for stock. Four typical discount rates are shown in the following table, with the publisher net, the distribution price minus the $3.09 printing charge for a 168 page paperback, shown for each level. At our 35% discount, Foner Books nets $6.63 per book sold through distribution.

Discount	55%	45%	35%	25%
Distribution Price	$6.73	$8.22	$9.72	$11.21
Printing Charge	$3.09	$3.09	$3.09	$3.09
Publisher Net	$3.64	$5.13	$6.63	$8.12

Self-Publishing

It's tough to beat self-publishing as a business model, but it carries the same stigma in some people's eyes as print-on-demand. If you're worried about how people will perceive your books, either don't use your family name as the publisher name or write under a pen name. That's literally the only difference between a self-publisher and any other kind of publisher, at least as far as the public can tell. The advantages of self-publishing in terms of author relations and minimizing out-of-pocket expenses are so obvious that there's no point dwelling on them. However, you have to be honest with yourself about how hard you're willing to work to start a publishing business and you have to be realistic about the probable outcome.

There are dozens of books about self-publishing which are replete with stories of rejected authors who strike it rich, but that type of success is incredibly rare and doesn't serve as a model you can follow. The average book published in the U.S. sells less than 2,000 copies in its lifetime, and since bestsellers and heavily promoted trade published books pull up that average, you had better believe that the average self-published book sells closer to 200 copies. Success in any type of publishing is dependent upon salesmanship, so if you aren't willing to invest at least as much time in selling your book as you invested in writing it, there's little reason to go into the publishing business.

The Role of Subsidy Publishing

Subsidy publishing, sometimes called vanity publishing since the author pays to get a book published, has always been a profitable business for subsidy publishers. They do fill an important function in the book world, however, and I've often recommended them to authors, depending on the circumstances. The adoption of POD by subsidy presses has allowed them to lower their charges to as little as $200 to have a no-frills book published. Many subsidy publishers use Lighting Source, ensuring that the book will be available through the Ingram distribution network and thus available through over 90% of U.S. bookstores, in addition to online booksellers. Lightning Source also supplies Baker&Taylor, and they appear to be moving in the direction of directly supplying the chains. The best reason for an author to turn to a subsidy publisher is if the author has written a book that isn't commercially viable, and lacks the desire, skills, or financing to take the self-publishing route.

Authors should be careful about the contracts offered by subsidy presses and should retain all rights to their book with the option to end the relationship at any time. Authors shouldn't rely on a subsidy press to edit, proofread or otherwise contribute to the quality of a manuscript, whatever the price charged, and should obtain these services directly from local freelancers.

Subsidy publishers, like trade publishers, do pay author royalties, and the royalty schedules offered by subsidy publishers are frequently higher than those offered by big trades. This is made possible by the fact that the subsidy publisher has financed the publication risk with the author's money, so any profits resulting from sales are gravy. Some subsidy publishers attempt to occupy a middle ground by basing their business model on both the author's contribution and profits from sales. These publishers are selective in the books they accept for publication and work with the author to create a quality product and are among the least expensive subsidy presses, charging as low as two or three hundred dollars to publish a book. An example of such a publisher is Booklocker, and their contract is available online for anybody to read at:

http://www.booklocker.com/contract/contract.txt

If you have a book that's not commercial enough for a trade publisher and all you want is to make it available to the public, then go with a reasonable subsidy press, and save yourself a lot of money and heartache.

Small Publisher Distribution

Distribution is a critical piece of the publishing puzzle, yet most new publishers seem to think it will magically open up to them once they publish a book. The only thing that will magically open up is the publisher's wallet. We talked a little about the two largest distributors, Ingram Books, which Lightning Source publishers get access to, and Baker&Taylor, with whom almost any publisher can sign up. However, Baker&Taylor doesn't automatically stock books for small publishers. When talking about distribution, it doesn't mean much unless the distributor keeps the publisher's books in stock. While in-stock status at a national distributor is essential to selling books in quantity through retail outlets, it can carry a heavy price. Distributors who deal with small publishers usually require a discount between 65% to 75% off the cover price. In other words, they pay the publisher between 25% to 35% of the cover price on books they actually sell. The books must be returnable, and they will often be returned in beat-up condition that renders them unfit for sale elsewhere. Smaller distributors sometimes go out of business, at which point the publisher's stock may end up at a remainder house, regardless of legal agreements to the contrary. Distributors may also play musical chairs with books, returning them all before payment is due and then accepting them again under a new payment schedule. Some distributors, whether or not they will actively promote the publisher's books, require a sizeable number of books for stock. Although this seems positive at first blush, it's a big risk for the publisher if any of the bad scenarios described above play out or if the book simply doesn't sell.

Most bookstores have direct computer access to the Ingram catalog, where they can find any book distributed by Ingram by the ISBN, title, author, without referring to "Books in Print." Many independent bookstores make Ingram their first stop, since there are benefits to ordering the maximum number of books from a single source. It's still critical for publishers to update their "Books in Print" record on BowkerLink when adding or changing a distributor, since this is the only way some customers can find out who distributes the book. One mission that all new publishers should undertake is to visit their local bookstores and find out which distributors they prefer and which distributors they don't work with. Many distributors really serve as consolidators for Ingram, who prefers not to deal directly with small imprints and even offers a list of the distributors they deal with on their website. Almost all distributors offer paid marketing programs to publishers, ranging from a few hundred dollars for a small ad in direct mailing or magazine, to thousands of dollars for a large space ads or other special treatment.

Another distribution option for small publishers is to be distributed by a larger publisher, even a multi-billion dollar trade press. One offer we received from a publisher who releases thousands of their own new titles each year was to distribute our books for a 70/30 split (with us getting the 70). Since our books are designed from the outset for print-on-demand, we weren't even tempted, but the economics are interesting. If the books were redesigned for offset printing and purchased in quantity, the printing cost would drop to around a dollar a book. However, what looks like a pretty healthy split is based on the net proceeds the publisher would receive for the book, selling it at the trade discount or a little higher. If books were sold for 55% off of our $14.95 cover price ($6.72), then we would receive 70% of that amount ($4.71), minus returns, shipping costs, and the cost of money for the big print run. Making only a minor allowance for the overhead costs, we'd actually earn around half as much per book as through POD publishing, and be running a financial risk in the bargain.

Internet Publication for Writers

The Internet has opened up an incredibly valuable publishing platform for writers. The business model we advocate in this book is built on Internet marketing through the website of the publisher or the author. Unfortunately, writers who lack Internet or publishing savvy may fall into the trap of unscrupulous Internet publishers who are looking for free content to draw visitors to their sites, or may even charge writers a fee for showcasing their work. Some of these online publishers even sign authors to contracts that effectively make the Internet publisher the prime beneficiary should the author ever find a trade publisher for the work. This practice is particularly effective with unpublished writers who understandably want to have something to show for their labor of love and will eagerly sign on the dotted line for the right to finally tell themselves that they have arrived. The current practice of many e-book publishers is similar to that of unpaid internships. However, unlike the unpaid internship which often carries the implied promise of a paid job offer on completion, or at least provides resume experience in some tough-to-break-into field, publication on most e-book sites returns nothing to the writer. The key to understanding the lack of value offered by many Internet e-book publishers is how little they actually invest in the work. An author who sends an online publisher a word processing file for conversion into an e-book or a web page should know that this process can be fully automated, literally not costing the "publisher" a dime or a keystroke.

The less ethical POD subsidy publishers are little better, though it's likely somebody will glance through the file their conversion template produces to make sure there's text on most of the pages. Cover designs for such books are produced from standard templates in a matter of minutes, and the large subsidy presses get discounts on any setup charges from printers. Authors who sign up with the wrong publisher can expect to see requests for advertising money to start coming in before the book is even printed. Some of these supposed publishers make the lion's share of their income selling marketing services to their clients, which aren't a bit more valuable than the original publication service.

Trade Published E-books

All major publishers have at least experimented with e-books, and most have been including the right to publish electronic versions of printed works in author contracts for at least the past ten years. Still, if you're a trade author and your book is officially out-of-print, it is definitely worthwhile to pull the contract out of the drawer and check the clause about how rights can revert to your ownership. If the publisher doesn't put the book back into print by making it available as print-on-demand, the author may recover rights to the book, even if the publisher filed the copyright. Anecdotal stories to the contrary, e-books are not generating serious money with old, trade published books. However, you might make $50 or $100 a month by republishing a popular out-of-print book as an Amazon e-doc with very little up-front cost.

A few years ago there were a large number of e-publishers who basically followed the procedures of a traditional publisher, except they only published e-books. The nonfiction publishers who stuck with e-books for professionals probably had the most success, but e-books failed to catch on with the majority of the reading public despite the massive free publicity the industry received in the early days. The inability of the industry to agree on Digital Rights Management (DRM), or to settle on a standard reader for e-books, whether a dedicated hardware reader or free software for a PC, didn't help any either. While e-book sales were up over 100% last year, they started from such a low level that it will take a few years of such growth before they begin generating serious interest again. One positive thing you can say about e-books is that it's fairly easy for POD publishers to take a title formatted as a PDF file for print-on-demand, change the ISBN, tweak them for screen resolution, and sell the PDF file as an e-book.

The main advantage to POD publishers in offering e-book versions of their titles is to increase availability. E-books sold through Amazon are available for download, world-wide, with no shipping costs or delays. This works particularly well with professional books, for which foreign language equivalents may not exist, extending the customer base for English language titles to non-native English speakers. When Foner Books released one of our titles in an e-book version a year after the print version was published, it generated $500 in profits the first two months. We've since released all of our titles as e-books through Lightning Source. E-books are an ideal way to meet demand from online impulse buyers, and publishers with strong Internet marketing will benefit the most from e-book sales.

Stepping Stones

Self-publishing can definitely serve as a stepping stone to trade publishing, providing you still want to go that route after having success as a self-publisher. There's nothing publishers love more than a sure thing, so a book with steadily increasing sales that's succeeding without the benefit of a trade publisher's backing is always a likely candidate. Publishers do shy away from niche books that have depended heavily on a single marketing channel, particularly if they believe that the market in question has already absorbed most of the demand. A book that can sell a couple of thousand copies a year on the backlist of a trade publisher will always be viewed as an asset, but they aren't going to get excited about acquiring a book they think will only sell a couple of hundred copies a year.

Whether or not you want to sell a successful self-published title and whether or not a trade publisher wants to buy it, you'll have something to put in your future book proposals aside from your participation in the local writer's club. Acquisitions editors love to hear from authors who are as knowledgeable about book marketing as they are ignorant about publishing contracts, and self-publishing a book is a great way to educate yourself. Print-on-demand is the best way to get into self-publishing because it solves the riddle that even the most experienced trade publishers can't answer, namely, how many books is a new title going to sell? Rather than tying up all of your cash and credit in boxes of books, not to mention every inch of available space in your home, you can run a business with no inventory. If you absolutely need the extra quality an offset press offers, buy the shortest print run you can, usually 100 copies, even if it means you'll barely break even selling the books. You can always order a larger print run if they start selling like hotcakes, and if your book is a runaway success, the minor hit to profits from the early break-even sales won't cost you a minute of sleep. On the other hand, thousands or tens of thousands of dollars of unsold books can cost you many sleepless nights and make it that much harder to pick yourself up and try again.

The Book Market

New publishers often publish books without giving much thought to where those books will eventually be sold. For example, the majority of new titles issued by small publishers will never be stocked by the chain superstores, not even for a three-month tryout. Only a tiny number of small publisher titles will ever be selected by discount merchandisers or the local supermarket for stocking in their book sections, yet these outlets actually account for a hefty percentage of industry book sales. It pays for a publisher to be realistic about the prospects for a new title to be stocked on store shelves, not only in terms of choosing between offset printing and print-on-demand, but also in terms of book design and production. There is always a limited amount of money available for the production and marketing of a new title, and the efficient allocation of that money to the different facets of the business can determine whether the publisher will live to publish another book.

Traditional Booksellers

Traditional booksellers include brick-and-mortar bookstores (an expression to describe physical retail locations in the Internet age), mail order book clubs, specialty shops, and mass merchandisers such as discount chains and supermarkets. Mass merchandisers and book clubs are simply out of reach for the vast majority of small publisher titles, which need to reach bestseller status to be considered. Distribution, as mentioned previously, is key to getting most independent bookstores and specialty stores to consider stocking your title, as their resources are too limited to deal with a large number of vendors. However, you don't need to be stocked by brick-and-mortar shops in order for them to sell your books. The key is to generate customer demand that leads to special orders.

The two dominant retail bookstore chains in the U.S. are Barnes&Noble and Borders. Data from their 2003 annual reports shows that the Barnes&Noble (along with their B. Dalton subsidiary) had $4.12 billion in sales, while Borders (with their Walden Books subsidiary) had $3.31 billion in North American sales. This combines for $7.43 billion in annual sales. Add $2.27 billion for Amazon (North America, includes CD's and DVD's), and $440 million for BN.com, and you get over $10 billion in sales coming from just these four outlets. Statistics on total industry book sales can be very misleading because they include a high proportion of educational sales and direct sales of professional and academic books to libraries. Likewise, the reported sales for bookstores often include some music, video, or other media sales. The combined sales from the Barnes&Noble and Borders chains alone accounts for over half of all retail bookstore sales, with much of the balance coming from religious or specialty shops and university bookstores, rather than independent books shops. Despite this, independent bookstores are a great outlet for special order books because of their focus on customer service and their willingness to go the extra mile in ordering. One advantage for bookstores in taking special orders from customers is that they get those customers into the store for both ordering and pickup, which presents two opportunities to sell them additional items.

The U.S. Census Bureau, which publishes some of the most reliable numbers you can find on anything, put 2003 bookstore sales as follows:

Sales Period	Millions $
January	$2,094
February	$1,005
March	$929
April	$984
May	$1,105
June	$1,179
July	$1,129
August	$2,083
September	$1,524
October	$1,065
November	$1,047
December	$2,036
Total	$16,180

Note that these numbers include university bookstores, which explains the high sales levels in January, August and September. Christmas sales account for the December bounce. College book sales throughout the year account for over $3 billion of the reported total, leaving approximately $13 billion for both general and specialty bookstores, which includes news stands, stationery shops, and religious and specialty booksellers.

Bookstore Modeling and Stocking

Store managers at bookstore chains have some leeway as to which books will be stocked in their local store. However, with the new superstores featuring up to 100,000 books at a single location, it's obvious that the majority of stocking decisions are made by the chain buyers and subsequent sales results. The buyers sometimes depend on the trade publishers themselves to determine which books to give a chance on the shelves, and despite the huge capacity of these stores, most titles in stock will be backlist or editions of older books, making competition for the remaining spots fierce indeed. On the other hand, trade publishers are very attentive to the demands of chain buyers and will sometimes change the design of a book to ensure that the chain will give it an opportunity on the shelves. A small and ever-shrinking number of independent bookstores will stock books from local authors or publishers on consignment in a special section for the sake of community relations.

The term "modeling" is used to describe how many copies of a particular title a store will stock. A book modeled for two copies means the store continually reorders to keep two copies on the shelf. For a chain to continue modeling a book, it needs to achieve average sales of more than one copy per store per year. However, that doesn't mean a chain will give a new title a whole year, or even six months, to start generating those sales. Bookstore chains use sophisticated computer models to analyze sales and predict stocking requirements on a continual basis, so a title that fails to show significant sales early on will disappear from the shelves within a few months. A chain with 500 superstores would want to see at least 10 copies per week sold across the chain to justify keeping the title in stock. Less than that, it's back to the chain's distribution center and from there a return ticket to the publisher. Some people are surprised that the superstores will stock a title that only sells a couple of copies per store per year, but part of the attraction of a superstore to consumers is the huge number of titles they stock. The chains may prefer to stock strictly fast-moving bestseller titles, but the slower-moving books provide "wallpaper" that's necessary for the ambiance. The best independent bookstores turn over their inventory more often than the chain stores, perhaps three times a year as compared to twice, but those numbers are inflated by bestsellers.

Online Booksellers

Everybody knows that the big dog of online book sales is Amazon.com, but they are far from being the only online retailer. Other notables include BN.com, Half.com, Alibris and Books-a-Million. Online book selling has brought a number of fundamental changes to the book business, including steep discounts on numerous new titles, and selling used books right alongside the new. Amazon even reminds customers they can resell the books they've bought from Amazon as used books in Amazon's Marketplace. In spite of all of the philosophical arguments offered by people who like to argue, there's no doubt that this wide availability of used books has hurt the bottom lines of both publishers and authors. The positive side of this is that it also allows publishers to bypass the entire distribution tangle and control their own pricing.

Amazon sold $2.27 Billion in books, music, and videos in 2003, or about half the sales of either of the major brick-

and-mortar chains. This represented a 14% growth over the previous year, a healthy trend, and the sales of new and used items (mainly books) through Amazon Marketplace and Z-Shops accounted for almost 1 in 4 items purchased through the Amazon site this year. This doesn't mean that 25% of book sales on Amazon result in no revenue for the author or publisher. Many of the books sold as new through the Marketplace are purchased through legitimate distribution by the vendors who turn a small profit on the discount spread and shipping and handling. It makes no difference to the income of a publisher or author whether the book is sold directly by Amazon or by one of these mega-middlemen, as long as the books aren't remainders or used copies.

Selling Books on Amazon

This section simply covers how you can sell your books through the world's largest bookstore. We'll get to marketing books on Amazon in the Internet Marketing chapter.

There are three basic ways for a small publisher to sell books through Amazon, the easiest of which is to let your distributor do it. Since our POD books are printed by Lightning Source, we get hands-off access to Amazon with no shipping charges incurred. Most distributors have relationships with Amazon, but some publishers, if their distributor hasn't signed them to an exclusive deal, may prefer to deal with Amazon directly through their Advantage program. Amazon Advantage allows publishers to have their books stocked by Amazon in return for a small yearly fee, the 55% trade discount, accepting returns, and paying for shipping. Advantage members get access to a special website with stocking and sales information for their titles, though the information on the regular Amazon site is usually more up-to-date.

Another option for selling your books through Amazon is to use their Marketplace or Z-Shops to take orders which you'll ship directly to customers. This type of transaction is accounting for an increasing proportion of Amazon sales, and it is a terrific business for Amazon since it doesn't have to handle the books. There are grades of sellers in this alternative channel, the simplest of which is the basic Marketplace account. With a valid credit card and checking account number, you can sign up online for free, which will allow you to sell unlimited titles as new or used, that will be available through the basic Amazon page for a title uniquely identified by the ISBN. The last time we used this method, Amazon charged a $0.99 listing fee (only if the item is sold) plus 15% percent of the sale price, and they also make a mark-up of the shipping and handling money they pass through to the seller. They e-mail a shipping label which you can print and tape to the package.

A step up from the basic Marketplace account is a Pro Merchant account. There is a fee ($39.95/month at the beginning of 2004), in return for which Amazon waves the $0.99 listing fee, but still takes a percentage of the sale price. Rather than listing books for sale one at a time, members of the Pro Merchant program can upload an entire inventory worth of data, which makes it especially valuable for small publishers who also happen to own a bookstore or distribute books for other small publishers. The Amazon inventory loader supports UIEE (Universal Information Exchange Environment), which is used by many third party database tools you can purchase to manage inventory for a bookstore. The Pro Merchant account also qualifies the seller for a Z-Shop storefront, a customizable online selling presence to which you can send people to directly, in addition to appearing in Amazon product searches.

Direct Sales

Many small publishers see direct sales as the plum of their operation, highly profitable with no outside dependencies. On the other hand, most large trades discourage direct sales, not even offering a discount through their websites, because they have optimized their operations over the years to sell books through distribution and lack the flexibility to include high-margin direct sales into their operations. Some small publishers use direct mail exclusively, selling books through the online booksellers and through their own websites, magazine ads, newsletters, etc. Some small publishers become so focused on direct sales that they don't even bother with an ISBN block, which effectively excludes their books from all online systems and renders them invisible as a publisher.

Effectively marketing books is the primary challenge for generating direct sales, but processing orders and shipping and handling deserve a mention as well. Many new publishers feel forced into credit card processing deals with merchant banks, including an initial layout of several hundred dollars for a terminal (swiper) or a lease deal with no escape clause and high monthly payments. In addition, most credit card processors charge monthly fees plus a small percentage of every sale. At Foner Books, we decided to stick with Internet-based solutions, with no up-front costs. Initially, we signed up as an Amazon Marketplace seller and let Amazon process the majority of our mail order sales. However, we didn't like the relatively high fees involved, and we had several requests from customers who wanted us to accept PayPal payments.

These customers either didn't have credit cards, didn't want to use them on the Internet, or were regular PayPal users who prefer keeping all their online purchases in one account. PayPal offers a simple refund procedure for when customers make mistakes or for the rare lost book, and adding PayPal processing to our website was as simple as filling out a form and pasting the code they sent onto our web page. PayPal also provides printable labels addressed to customers with prepaid Media Mail postage and tracking. We also accept personal checks for books, though this never amounted to a significant proportion of sales, and we stopped advertising the fact just to streamline the ordering instructions. For in-state orders, we charge a 5% sales tax, and our PayPal account is set up to do this automatically. I honestly believe that if PayPal had been available when my first Internet site made it possible for me to sell books direct, I never would have signed up with a trade publisher.

Special Sales

If a potter who routinely exhibits at craft fairs wants to buy 50 copies of your "Modeling Presidents in Clay" title in hopes that selling them will cover the cost of the booth, this is termed a "special sale." In the Internet age, it's important to realize that you shouldn't discount books to get quantity orders unless you're confident that those books won't come back to compete with your own direct sales. We've received requests from fledgling entrepreneurs who wanted us to sell them books at a discount so they could resell them on the Internet. We don't need a middleman to sell our books online and certainly wouldn't pay (through a higher discount) for the privilege. Anybody who contacts us looking for a quantity deal for any purpose is offered the same 35% discount we assign through Lightning Source and is invited to prepay for the order so we don't get stuck with inventory.

International Sales

Selling books overseas is a really tough game for small publishers. Foner Books gets U.K. distribution through Lighting Source U.K., but our only other international sales come through direct mail, which involves pricing the mailing charges separately for each country. While we've found that customers in places as far as Australia and Africa are willing to pay shipping charges that exceed the prices of our books, we prefer sending them to Amazon so we don't have to set up a payment mechanism for all the different shipping rates. The only real option to overseas direct mail for a small publishing business is either setting up a relationship with a distributor in each country and shipping books internationally, or setting up with a print-on-demand provider who has partners in many countries. This amounts to quite a bit of work, expense, and risk in trusting the foreign distributor to stay in business and pay their bills. Unless a small publisher has a large number of titles in print or a particular title that has strong appeal in one overseas market or another, the risks probably outweigh the potential benefits.

Shipping books in quantity overseas is a highly risky business, and one that I'd only engage in on a prepaid basis. The Internet has given rise to some incredibly imaginative schemes in which con artists from other countries will order books from American companies in an attempt to catch the publisher in a standard banking scam. One popular approach is to send the publisher a cashiers check on a foreign bank that is "accidentally" drawn for an amount a few hundred or thousand dollars above the transaction cost. The publisher is then asked to refund the difference with a cashiers check drawn on the publisher's bank, only to find after it's sent that the foreign check is forged or invalid. If they're out to steal your books and not your money, they can simply use a stolen credit card, and you'll find it impossible to get your books back. The safest way to accept money from overseas is by a wire transfer, and you should confirm with your bank that the money has arrived and been irrevocably deposited in your account before you ship the books.

Foreign Rights Sales

One way around the problems of international distribution is to sell foreign publishers the right to publish and distribute a title in their country. The big trade publishers with subsidiary companies in every country that has a bookstore only sell foreign rights when a translation is involved; even then, they may have their local subsidiary do the work. From the standpoint of a small publisher, selling foreign rights is an expensive proposition because such sales usually take place at international book shows, like the annual fair in Frankfurt, Germany. It also means paying for some lawyer time, preferably a lawyer with experience in international intellectual property law, which isn't going to come cheap. It also entails all of the risks inherent in dealing with another business, particularly if the rights sale is based on a royalty sharing scheme, rather than a one-time payment.

Perhaps the greatest risk in a foreign rights sale for a small publisher is competition on the Internet, whether or not the contract includes any electronic rights. The major trade publishers can afford litigation to protect their rights should a foreign partner violate contract terms, but a small publisher almost certainly cannot. If a publisher or a publisher's employee in Europe or Asia decides to put the full text of your book on the web in order to boost their traffic or to attract buyers to their legally licensed version or translation, it could kill your own website. It also increases the likelihood of your stumbling across a CD being sold online in the U.S. that contains your book in an electronic library or something similar. The best protection is to only deal with foreign companies that are highly reputable and have been around for a long time, and then only with the advice of a good lawyer.

Bookseller Attitudes towards POD

You might think that bookstore employees would be open-minded, thoughtful and supportive of authors and publishers. Yet when I ordered a POD book written by a friend of mine at the classiest independent bookstore in town, the clerk couldn't help commenting, "Oh, print-on-demand. That's for writers who can't get published." For my part, I couldn't keep myself from pointing out that the book in question was by an author with over a dozen trade published books who chose to set up his own publishing company so he could actually earn a living, but I don't think the clerk was impressed. Unfortunately, print-on-demand has become synonymous with subsidy publishing in the minds of many book industry professionals, and that's unlikely to change any time soon.

Bookstores who special order books are no less willing to order POD books than any other kind. What does impact a bookstore's willingness to order a title is whether or not it's returnable, what the assigned discount is, and whether or not it's in stock. Bookstores that don't ask customers to prepay for special orders often find that those customers never return to buy the book. Some bookstores, even some stores that are part of larger chains, won't order books unless they actually show as "in stock" at a warehouse shown on their computer screen. It's tough to blame stores for not wanting to order books if they aren't sure when they'll arrive, so it's critical to get a distributor who will keep your books in stock and not just order them from you or your printer when they have a customer. Ingram may show virtual inventory for Lightning Source books, since they can be printed, received at Ingram and shipped in less than 24 hours.

Market Research

Whether you are an author or a publisher, the most crucial decision you have to make on a recurring basis is selecting your next book. We look at title selection through the filter of what's possible with print-on-demand, since that's what this book is all about. The overriding factor to keep in mind when thinking about new POD titles, especially for the nonfiction market, is the relatively poor photographic reproduction available from the commercial POD printers. You might find a boutique printer using special equipment that can even do a decent job on color interiors, but they will be very expensive, and may also lack the distribution ties that are so critical for success. Many nonfiction publishers, especially of how-to books, rely heavily on photographs as part of the narrative and to bulk up page count. When considering new titles, try thinking of the subject matter from a fresh perspective. In working around the photographic limitations, you may develop a unique title (something major trade publishers hate to gamble on) that has competitive advantages of its own. For example, we recently published a POD computer repair book, a subject that traditionally depends heavily on photo illustrations, frequently employing more than one photo a page. The repair book that was eventually written for POD publication didn't contain a single photograph. A series of troubleshooting flowcharts provided the visual core for the book, since black and white line drawings work quite nicely with toner based printing.

Publish What You Know You Can Sell

There's no more true or succinct advice for new authors in any genre than the old adage, "Write what you know." For publishers, I've taken the liberty of adding a couple of words, "Publish what you know you can sell." If the great American novel walks through the door of your cookbook publishing company, you had better think twice and three times about how you're going to market that novel and justify the advance the great American novelist will no doubt expect. No successful business adds new products to the mix at random, just because the quality is high or the price is right. Expanding your horizons is always a good idea, both professionally and personally, but in the publishing business, you had better have a marketing plan.

The most frequently overlooked component of a book marketing campaign is the determination of whether or not a market for that title exists. It's occasionally possible to create a market for a new title where none existed before, since every new genre in publishing begins with such a breakthrough, but it doesn't happen every day. The safest marketing bet for any publisher or author is to target their next title for the same market as their last success. Not a competing title, but a complimentary work, one that would appeal to both customers and resellers of the previous book.

Even if you're writing or publishing groupings of closely related nonfiction books, it's difficult to determine when the market is saturated. A parallel between book publishing and the stock market is that nobody, not even the insiders, can predict with certainty when the bubble is going to burst.

New titles can dilute the presence of the original, causing them all to disappear from the shelves or fall off the radar screen at Amazon. A typical trade publisher will follow up a bestselling title "How to Grow Tomatoes" with "How to Grow Plum Tomatoes", "How to Grow Organic Tomatoes" and "How to Grow Cherry Tomatoes." There may be a market for the books, especially if the previous series on "How to Grow Peppers" went into five editions with successful offshoot titles on "Chile Peppers", "Decorative Peppers" and "Diet Peppers." You can't blame publishers for trying, but I wouldn't bet the ranch dressing.

Market Research

For most publishers, market research consists of data mining, culling through their own sales data or industry wide data obtained from distributors or subscription services. Imitation really is the sincerest form of flattery in the publishing business, though most authors who've been "flattered" through knock-off titles would have preferred a kind word. Large trade publishers may fool around with focus groups before launching a new initiative, but it would be difficult to justify that sort of overhead cost for an individual title. Publishers will send acquisitions editors to industry events and professional conferences to try to spot hot areas and growing trends, but most new titles are still brought in by authors. As a small publisher or author, there are five free market research tools just waiting for you to take advantage.

1) Bookstore Shelves

I spend a lot of time in bookstores and libraries, and there's plainly a relationship between books consistently appearing on these shelves and actual demand over time. Bookstores, if they are large enough, are a pretty good place keep an eye on mainstream books, but it can be difficult to separate the steady earners from the wallpaper titles. I always check the printing number on the copyright page when I look at books in a store. If a book was published in the last twelve months and it's already in a third or higher printing, that's a strong indication it's selling well. Backlist books stocked by the chains should also go through at least one printing a year. Keep in mind, however, that some pretty strong books don't get stocked for a variety of reasons, especially those from smaller publishers who focus on other distribution methods. Stores can also be slow to stock successful new titles, depending on the season and publisher promotions.

2) Library Books

You can measure demand for a library book by checking the wear-and-tear or the number of date stamps, if your library hasn't modernized beyond stamping due dates in books. Unfortunately, this only works for books that are popular enough to be acquired, not popular enough to have been stolen, and which happen to be on the shelf when you visit. Still, if you visit the library on a regular basis, it pays to keep an eye on the subject sections in which you publish. Library collections tend to go light on how-to books (which usually do get stolen when acquired), and they also prefer hardcovers to paperbacks. Still, if you're an author or a publisher who wants to publish books with staying power, library availability is a great way to separate the crazes from the trends.

3) Published Bestseller Lists

Everyone publishes bestseller lists, from the big newspapers to the big distributors—even the independent bookstores club their data to generate a list. All of these lists suffer from being too narrow in scope, but that's the penalty when you pick the top 10 or 25 of anything. There's also the little matter of the positive feedback loop they generate that works to keep an existing "bestseller" on the list and may actually hurt chances for a similar title. Published bestseller lists are only valuable for detecting very broad trends, but you can generate an almost infinite number of custom bestseller lists on Amazon, which we'll talk about in detail later in the chapter.

4) Online Interest

There are lots of ways to determine the online interest in a subject, aside from looking at Amazon or Barnes&Noble.com sales ranks. You can look at the number of public discussion groups and the level of activity in those groups on Yahoo!, Google, or the newsgroups. You can do simple searches on Google and note the raw number of websites that come up for a key phrase. While online interest won't necessarily translate into book sales, it's a pretty good indication that the subject has an audience outside the author and the publisher. If you have the flexibility to engineer your book title, Internet keyword testing beats focus groups for both cost and honesty.

5) Proprietary Data

Publishers can subscribe to services that track book sales at the point of sale or purchase publishing reports outright, but this is a serious expense that small publishers should avoid. If you have your own data from titles you've published, that's the most accurate measure of demand you can find, and it gives you a way to calibrate the sales of other titles that are grouped around yours in terms of online sales ranks or positions in bestseller sorts. The largest U.S. book distributor is Ingram, and you can get their sales numbers for a given ISBN through their automated stock check and sales tool at (615) 213-6803. They limit you to 5 title checks per call. The problem with using Ingram numbers is in estimating what percentage of the title's sales goes through Ingram. That's a tall task, because it depends on how strong the publisher is at direct sales to both consumers and bookstores, who else distributes the book, and where the majority of the sales come from (i.e., independent book stores, chains, supermarkets, specialty stores).

Amazon Sales Ranking

I call Amazon the "free market" of bookstores, simply because they "shelve" most in-print titles, and make it easy (if not always highly profitable) for the small publishers to play. As with the other methods for gauging demand we reviewed above, there are some peculiarities to the Amazon data; first and foremost that they sell by mail order. This causes titles that do well front-and-center in bookstores, including eye-candy and impulse buy books, to be under-weighted by Amazon data. On the other end of the spectrum, titles not stocked in bookstores will be over-weighted in Amazon data, since the majority of sales for that book could be generated online. There's no doubt a broad spectrum of the American book-buying public shops for titles of all genres at Amazon, making it the best one-stop source for publicly available book industry information. Note that the following analysis of Amazon sales ranks is unauthorized and in no way sponsored by Amazon. It represents my personal observations and estimates based on six years of closely following the sales ranks of my own books as both an author and a publisher, and data points other authors and publishers have shared with me over the years. A more detailed and up-to-date description of ranks along with a curve for estimating the daily sales for any given rank is posted on our website at:

http://www.fonerbooks.com/surfing.htm

Every book that has sold at least one copy at Amazon is automatically assigned a sales rank. This number can range anywhere from #1 for the latest blockbuster to the low millions for a book that has sold a single copy, and no two books are assigned the same sales rank at the same time. This means that the many titles which have all sold just one copy through Amazon or tie at some other equal number of sales are further ranked within a range by some arbitrary measure, like first-come first-serve, or alphabetical order. There are three distinct ranking schemes on Amazon: one for the top selling 10,000 books, another for the books between 10,000 and 100,000, and a third for ranks above 100,000. Confusing the issue is the fact that these schemes overlap, and the one that yields the best rank wins out. Above all, sales ranks are only significant when they remain in the same range for an extended period of time, weeks or months. If the sales rank for a book is in the top 10,000 when you look one day, but above a hundred thousand when you check the next week, it's the higher number (worse rank) that really describes the current sales.

Books with sales ranks between 1 and 10,000 are re-ranked every hour. The rank depends both on how many books sold the previous hour relative to all the other books on Amazon, plus the recent sales trajectory. A book that holds steady in this range is usually considered commercially viable by trade publishers. Since ranks are relative and overall book sales vary with the time of year, there is no exact formula for describing a sales rate. Books with a steady sales rank near 10,000 are averaging sales of more than one copy a day. Around a sales rank of 1,000, the sales rate approaches ten copies a day. Keep in mind that some of these ranks are occupied by books that sold many thousands of copies on Amazon during their day in the sun, and hold onto a good sales rank for years because that initial surge of sales keeps their "average" above that of most other books. Books with steady sales ranks below 1,000 are selling very well, topping several dozen copies a day as you approach 100. I don't have any hard data on the top 100 books, but I'm sure it puts a smile on the face of any trade publisher to have a book selling that well, independent of the season and the competition.

Books in the range from 10,000 to 100,000 are re-ranked once a day in relation to all the other books on Amazon. Any book that sells a couple of copies a week for a couple of months after coming out will work its way into the top 100,000 for a time, but keep in mind that Amazon is merely predicting a rank based on the current sales momentum. It's this predictive component that allows a new edition of a popular book to quickly earn a sales rank higher than an earlier edition, even though the earlier edition has racked up far more actual sales. Books that sell a couple of copies a week over the course of a couple of years will earn pretty steady ranks in the middle of this range, and those ranks will deteriorate very slowly as sales tail off.

If the book has been hanging around in the top 100,000 for just a few months and its sales rate begins falling off, it will slowly drop towards 100,000, then jump from the high 90,000's to the mid-hundreds of thousands overnight. This final spot, which is extremely stable, is based on the total number of copies sold over the life of the book or the number of years Amazon has been tracking ranks, whichever is shorter. A stable rank just over 100,000 translates into total sales of about 250 books. A rank just above a million indicates total sales of approximately a dozen books. Ranks in this range aren't recomputed every day. A single additional sale for a book ranked above two million that has only sold one copy can improve the ranking by 500,000. In the area just under a million, each additional sale will improve the rank by around 30,000.

Amazon is not immune to the seasons and holidays that affect sales at all bookstores. If your titles don't have any holiday or gift appeal, their sales ranks will fall between Thanksgiving and Christmas, even if the actual sales remain steady. Likewise, university students buy a huge number of textbooks and other required reading titles through Amazon during September and from mid-January through mid-February, which will depress the ranks of books that don't fall into this category. If you become addicted to watching Amazon sales ranks, you'll see that they even vary in a regular manner during the course of the week. Some titles are primarily purchased by people at work or homemakers when the kids are at school, while books with strong Associates support do relatively well on weekends.

Amazon Browse Category Bestseller Lists

Another tool for determining the relative success of titles sold through Amazon is through their category lists. Amazon assigns books with substantial sales (or persistent publishers) to **Subject Categories**, which are listed near the bottom of the page for any give book under the heading:

Look for similar books by subject:
Browse for books in:

Each list starts with the word **subject**, followed by a category, subcategory, and often several subdivisions after that. Some lists may contain just a couple dozen books, while others encompass tens of thousands. The keywords in the **Browse for books in:** and the **Search for books by subject:** classifications associated with a book are taken into account when Amazon generates search results. Once you click on a category to get the listings, the new window offers the options **Featured, Recommendations, New Releases** and **Top Sellers**. These can also be reached through the **Sort By** box that appears just above the first book cover on the list. The bestseller lists for categories are not generated in real-time, or at least, they aren't generated from real-time sales ranks. The rankings in these bestseller lists appear to change every few days, though if there are no new strong sellers in the category, they may remain to be carved in stone over long periods of time.

The lists aren't foolproof. Some lucky titles get stuck in the top spots of a list and never budge, even if they've been outsold by any number of books in the category. This means you should always click on the top ten books in any bestseller list and look at their sales ranks. If they are really out of whack with the list order, check again the next week and the week after that. If, for example, you see a book with a sales rank worse than 50,000 consistently ranked above a bunch of books with sales ranks under 10,000, just ignore the anomaly. It takes a little time to develop a feel for how these lists actually work, so don't try doing all of your homework in one night, or you're likely to come up with the wrong answers.

Amazon Custom Bestseller Sorts

Custom bestseller lists can be generated directly from the standard Amazon search box or via the screen accessed through the search tab. However, since the addition of **Search Inside** to their site, the resulting bestseller sort may not be very useful, since it will probably include innumerable books that contain your search phrase. Instead, click on the **Search** tab to get a form that supports a set of choices, including **Author**, **Title**, **Subject**, **ISBN** and **Publisher**, and you can use one or more keywords in any of these (except ISBN) to narrow the scope. The idea is to be as specific as you can be while not excluding relevant results.

Another useful field when generating lists is the **Publication Date**. If you want to check what's selling for a rival (or friendly) publisher, just put the publisher name in the **Publisher** box, the current year in the **Publication Date** box, and select **Bestselling** in the **Sort Results By** box. It's also a good way for authors to check how their books are doing relative to other books their publisher has brought out.

The **Power Search** is my favorite Amazon feature. You can fill in the form to generate bestseller lists for Boolean searches, such as multiple publishers. I occasionally run a sort on the big POD subsidy publishers and include our little Foner Books, because we usually have one or two books in the top 10 on a bestseller list of over 28,000 books. I just put the following query in the **Power Search** box and sort the results by **Bestselling:**

publisher: (1stbooks or xlibris or iuniverse or foner)

Note: 1stBooks was renamed AuthorHouse in 2004.

All of these techniques give you the relative strength of a given title versus other related titles on Amazon. If you want to get an idea of how big the market is in the absolute sense, in other words, the total number copies a given title sells in a year, you can start from the sales that the chart on the FonerBooks.com website predicts based on the Amazon sales rank. Just make sure you check the ranking over the course of a few weeks to eliminate sales bubbles and temporary glitches at Amazon, and don't even bother unless the title is in the top 100,000.

Once you have a sales estimate for Amazon, you can make an educated guess as to what percentage of the title's total sales are through Amazon and extrapolate. If the title is modeled at one or two copies by the big chains, I'd multiply the Amazon sales rank estimate by five. If the book is also carried by independents, specialty shops and book clubs, I'd multiply by ten. If the book isn't stocked anywhere, but is available through Ingram, I'd multiply by two. Keep in mind that this reflects domestic U.S. sales for moderately selling books only. If a book is piled up at the front of every bookstore or in the aisles of mass merchandisers, the Amazon sales rank isn't going to be very useful for an absolute estimate.

Book Design

Just because you're a small publisher doesn't mean you have to do all the work yourself. Freelance professionals are available for all phases of book production, and can save you the expense of doing everything twice. An experienced cover designer can produce an original cover for $200 or less, as long as you're willing to accept their basic design scheme. Professional page compositors are far more expensive, costing anywhere from hundreds to thousands of dollars for an average size book. A reasonable hourly rate for a page compositor/book designer is in the $30-$40/hr range. Don't go with somebody who charges $5-$10 per page, that's just a formula for high costs. After the initial book design is created, the text is poured in and an experienced operator will only need a couple of minutes per page. A good page compositor will pick a suitable font, balance the pages, and make sure that the headers and footers are attractive and not crowded.

Paper weight, type and color are other important physical characteristics. The higher the paper weight, the better the quality. There are two standard systems for determining paper weight. One is used for the standard bond papers you buy for your copy machine or laser printer, the other is used by printers. To translate the familiar 20# or 24# weight you are familiar with to printer weights, multiply by 2.5. The 20# weight is equivalent to a 50#

printer weight, the 24# weight is equivalent to the 60# printer weight. Either weight is fine for trade paperbacks. Mass market paperbacks often use much lighter weight recycled paper, earning the name "pulp fiction." Once you pick the paper type, another number will fall out of this, the number of pages per inch (ppi). This is an important figure for cover designers, since the thickness of the binding obviously contributes to the size of the cover. Divide the number of pages in your book by the ppi, and you'll get the thickness of your book minus the cover.

Designing for Online Sales

With the rise of online bookstores, it's more important for most POD books (which will never see the inside of a bricks-and-mortar store) to have a cover that shows up well as a thumbnail on a web page than to be a visual knock-out from across the room. For nonfiction books, the title should be easy to read, and any cover illustration should have something to do with the book topic. I don't know what makes fiction sell, and I'm not going to pretend that I do. If you look at the book covers of successful POD publishers on Amazon, the main thing they have in common is simplicity of design. Many opt for a few colors with crisp titles and subtitles or a single hand-drawn graphic. You'll rarely see photographs or collages on these books. The potential benefit of getting such a cover to come out nicely isn't worth the downside of having it come out poorly. That's the real secret to designing your own books. Don't overreach. Simple and clean beats busy and complicated every time.

Designing book interiors doesn't scare most people as much as designing covers, but if you want positive word-of-mouth, getting the inside right is far more important than the cover. Don't make the book difficult to read in an attempt to make it stand out. There's no shame in looking at the design of books that you like and imitating them. This is what professional book designers have been doing since the beginning of time.

Page layout doesn't require learning expensive new software packages or complicated freeware work-arounds. If you're going to do page layout and book design for a living, by all means invest in Adobe InDesign or QuarkXPress. But for anyone doing their first book, stick with Microsoft Word or the word processor of your choice. We'll talk about creating PDF files a little later on, but the truth is, if you can make your book look right on your laser printer, you can stop right there. Most printers, including print-on-demand printers, can scan or photograph your clean laser printer copy and produce a book that, in the case of POD, will probably be indistinguishable from a book printed from a PDF. You'll be giving up some resolution that adds "snap" to the text if you use laser printed pages as the photo ready copy for an offset printer, but a $400 laser printer at 1200 dpi with the quality set to the highest level does a darn good job.

We recently produced a very complicated book straight out of Word and were amazed to learn that Word can place graphics on a page to the 1/100th of an inch. The indexing and table of contents generation in Word is superior to most desktop publishing packages, and the headers and footers combined with section breaks allow you to format the whole book in a single file with different chapter headers. Believe it or not, you can easily produce a book cover in PowerPoint or any other program that supports large paper sizes and basic drawing and text functions. This is all stuff you can learn, and I recommend a short guide by Aaron Shepard, "Books, Type, and Microsoft Word."

If you don't have Microsoft Word or freeware expertise and don't want to buy a desktop publishing package, your local copy shop probably has a few well-equipped PCs which they rent by the hour. My local Kinkos has both PCs and Macs, not to mention plenty of Postscript printers, which are important for checking your PDF output if you go that route. Whether the rental is $10/hour or $20, you'll be surprised to find how quickly the whole job goes if you come in knowing how you want the final product to look. It's also a great investment in time for anybody with a serious desire to work in the publishing business, even if you don't plan to spend your career typesetting books and designing covers. Once you've done it yourself, you'll have the vocabulary and the reference frame to discuss work with freelancers and to quickly spot the frauds.

Targeting the Market

The absolute first question you have to ask yourself is whether or not you're targeting bookstore sales. This book is an example of a book written and designed from the outset for online, direct mail and special order sales. By conceding bookstore shelving from the outset, we gained the flexibility to produce a low page-count book that a trade publisher would otherwise have bulked up with long appendices of reference information that's both easily found and more up-to-date online. Just for an experiment, try putting this book in the middle of a shelf in your home between a bunch of other paperbacks and imagine whether or not you'd have spotted it if you were browsing in a bookstore. The low page count also allows us to keep the cost down while using Lightning Source for zero inventory production and distribution.

Cookbooks and hobby books are a good example of market areas with special design considerations. For starters, many of these books work best with a spiral binding, so they can be laid flat for easy reading in the work area. Color will be a 100% requirement for some of these books, along with glossy or other special paper stocks not usually available with print-on-demand. However, it's even possible to do a very nice cookbook with POD. I saw an example that used black and white line drawings to break up the recipes, but it takes some extra creativity on the part of the author or designer. If you're looking for design ideas that don't use color printing or excessive numbers of photographs, just go to your local library and look for older books in the genre. Color printing once required special plates and inserts, adding significantly to the printing and binding cost for books, and even today, domestic printers charge a stiff premium for color printing.

What the ultimate selling price of the book will be is obviously a huge design consideration. Whether you stick with print-on-demand or go with an offset printer, the more pages there are in the book, the higher you'll have to set the cover price to earn a profit. Hard cover reference books are usually priced in the $50 to $150 range, and they usually try to provide one-stop shopping for a whole field of knowledge. If you can target just a portion of that field with an inexpensive paperback, you can tap into consumers who just aren't willing to spend $100 on an all-inclusive reference. Sometimes you may want to differentiate yourself from competing titles by publishing an expensive and weighty tome in a field that's dominated by handbooks. Do your market research and your math before you start, so you or your author has an idea approximately what length the book will be for a given binding, printing method and content.

Titling

Authors and publishers alike frequently mistake book titling as the ultimate challenge for expressing a theme through allegory. That works well for fiction titles that are backed by a big promotion budget, but for everybody else, the title had better say what the book is about in the clearest terms possible. Book searches, whether online, in your bookstore, or at the local library, are driven by the title, even if there's an annotation featuring a short essay about the contents. The reason for this is simple, and it applies to titling web pages as well as books. With the incredible amount of information available in even the most limited database system, the default method for sorting matches is based on the title. In bookstores, the part of the book that entices shoppers to take it off the shelf for a serious look is the title or author name on the spine. If I had titled this book, "Thought, Laser and Toner: From Neurons to Print and Back Again," the odds are that nobody would ever find it.

Trying to brand your books with catchy subtitles means giving up valuable keywords that could have been used to raise your title near the top of search results at bookstores, whether online or via a distributor database at a bookstore. The original subtitle of our case study book, "The Unembellished Guide," was a misguided attempt to create a brand. While the title, "Start Your Own Computer Business" was right on target, it wouldn't appear for searches such as "Start a PC Business" or "Computer Repair

Business." In addition, I'd missed the opportunity to tell customers more about the book, right in the subtitle. As shown in the case study numbers, our sales rose appreciably when we changed the subtitle to "Building a Successful PC Repair and Service Business by Supporting Customers and Managing Money." It's a real mouthful, but it does a much better job of telling potential customers what the book is about, and it contains many of the key words and phrases they might search under. The words don't have to be right next to each other or in the proper order to generate a strong result in a database search, meaning the book comes out near or on the top of the pile for a search phrase like "Computer Service and Repair."

Editing and Proofreading

Most writers do a poor job editing themselves, even if they are excellent editors when working on other authors' books. Some of us are so bad that we can actually pay attention to the grammar warnings the word processor gives! People refer to edits with a mix of terminology, which I'm going to reduce to three basic categories: copy edits, hard edits, and tech edits. All editing should be done on double spaced paper, with a red pen, even if the editor will be entering those changes into a manuscript using a **track changes** option.

A copy edit is basically one step up from proofreading. Where the scope of the proofreader is generally limited to spotting typographical errors, misspellings and really gross errors in presentation, the copy editor adds grammar to the mix. One of my own special sins is using split infinitives, and when the copy editor catches them, I often change them back. Copy editors generally follow a set of hard and fast rules about punctuation and word usage, and they don't pay a lot of attention to the overall structure of your composition or even the meaning of a sentence. You can give a copy editor a page of text written by a college English professor and get it back with three or four changes on every line! In other words, copy editors find their niche in bringing manuscripts in line with big publisher guidelines. Copy editors for large trades typically enforce gender neutral, politically-correct agendas, with maybe some cookie-cutter style guidelines thrown in. Due to the unfortunate fact that copy editors, particularly in the word processor age, often introduce errors, inexperienced publishers are probably better off skipping the copy edit and getting multiple proofreaders for the money.

A hard edit is when the editor is asked to improve the manuscript. This isn't cheating on the author's part, it's an honest admission that it's impossible to read your own work through somebody else's eyes. While a copy editor or a proofreader can do their work one sentence at a time, a hard editor should read the whole book through once before trying to edit it. Among the vague guidelines I gave my editor the first time I hired her, I asked her to make sure I didn't repeat myself. Her feedback, after reading the book, was "You don't repeat yourself enough!" The hard edit can result in suggestions to combine or eliminate major threads in the book, to add more explanatory text in some places, and to return to college and take an English course. Wholesale rework of paragraph structure is also common, and a hard edit often ends up including most of the benefits of a copy edit in one shot. Again, no editing is a substitute for proofreading on a finished, typeset, proof copy. It's just too easy to introduce mistakes when actually rewriting text or moving words around.

A technical edit is somewhat akin to fact checking and, depending on the manuscript, can end up being exactly the same thing. Some technical edits go far beyond simply reading a text with an expert eye and picking out flaws in logic or out-and-out mistakes. Technical editors of computer books, for example, are required to verify computer code in the book and on any accompanying CD. Technical editors (like myself) will often chip in with, "You're explaining it all wrong" or "That's a really dumb thing to be telling people." The technical editors on poorly written books often turn into de-facto co-authors. Not all nonfiction requires a technical edit and technical editing is not limited to "technical" subjects. For example, a cookbook editor who spots a recipe calling for a half cup of salt instead of a half-cup of sugar, or cooking a turkey two minutes for each pound, is essentially performing a technical edit. Technical editors must be experts in their field, not in English grammar.

Proofreading should be performed by a number of good readers, the more who fit your production schedule, the merrier. The manuscript should be given to proofreaders in the final, typeset, form. Aside from the possibility of errors being introduced by whomever does the typesetting, it's just easier for most people to pick out errors in a text that looks like a real book instead of double-spaced paper. Proofreaders should really restrain themselves from commenting on iffy grammar and stick to mistakes. Don't hesitate to use the "Search" option in your word processor to check every instance of words the author frequently confuses. In my case I check for "it's" or "its" and "who's" or "whose." I've never read a published book without finding some errors, and this book was no exception. POD allows you to occasionally update the text to chase out typos.

PDF Generation

When you hear PDF (Portable Document Format), you should think Adobe Acrobat, the original PDF viewer. The full version of Acrobat (as opposed to the free reader) produces PDFs as well. I don't own a copy myself, I'm waiting until I buy one of the publishing packages from Adobe, which lump together a couple thousand dollars (retail) of their software for $999. In the meantime, I've been producing PDFs with the freeware Ghostscript and GSView, which can be found online at:

http://www.cs.wisc.edu/~ghost/doc/AFPL/get800.htm

Ignore the silly advice you'll see on the web to just install any old Postscript printer driver and print to file, converting the results with Ghostscript. Download the Acrobat Distiller drive from Adobe (free) at:

http://www.adobe.com/support/downloads/main.html

And follow the install instructions to the letter. If you have your Word file just the way you like it and you don't plan on designing another book interior again any time soon, you can use the free trial Adobe offers (up to five conversions) instead of fooling around with setting up local PDF creation:

https://createpdf.adobe.com/index.pl

There's a learning curve involved in book production, but you're going to have to go through it whether you do all the work yourself or pay somebody else. Don't try to outsource any design decisions, both you and whomever you hire will just end up unhappy. Bite the bullet now, save yourself a few thousand dollars, and do it yourself.

Proof Checklist

Once your manuscript is finalized and your book design is completed, you send the electronic files off to an offset or print-on-demand printer. They'll either give you the option to pay a few bucks extra for a "proof" or "galley" print for final inspection, or send one for free as part of their process. TAKE THE TIME TO READ IT. I don't think I've made every mistake you can possibly make publishing books, but I'll probably get there eventually. I have made a couple thousand dollars in "skipped inspection" mistakes in my self-publishing career, so the following checklist is based on experience.

Cover – Yes, you've seen the cover a hundred times, probably approved a final version from a cover designer or artist already, but check it again. Make sure the title is spelled right, make sure it's centered on the book properly and you aren't losing some of the image over the edges. Make sure the ISBN number on the back is the correct one for your book. Same for the price. Proofread the back cover text a final time.

Spine – I blew this one myself to the tune of $900. My cover designer misspelled a word in the book's title on the spine, and I didn't catch it until the book jackets were printed. Make sure the spine text is centered on the spine and not creeping onto one of the covers.

Book Jacket (Hardcover) – Hardcover book jackets with inside flaps must be proofread again. I have a typo in the back flap text of that same hardcover jacket that I redid for the spine typo. I couldn't justify redoing it again for two repeated words in the flap text, but it still bothers me. Make sure that the case-binder or whoever is producing the actual cover of the hardcover gets the title on the spine correct as well.

Margins and fonts – Make sure the margins in the proof agree with the margins in your design. I have a book where they don't; fortunately the margins were large enough that the text didn't disappear into the binding. Make sure the fonts are the ones you selected, and more importantly, that they look nice. Check the top and bottom as well, with a ruler. If you find a mistake, don't be surprised if the printer tells you not to worry about it because the equipment they use for one-off isn't the same as the equipment they use for production. However, get your objection on record so if the real book is screwed-up, you won't have to pay for it.

Headers and footers – I had to halt production of a POD book after I had already approved it because I missed typos introduced by the book designer in the headers of two chapters. Since a header error appears on every other page in the chapter, or throughout the book, it's too serious of an error to pass on. While this didn't cost me any cash, it did cost me several hundred dollars in cancelled sales. The experience helped push me into doing my own book designs, as I'm perfectly capable of making such mistakes without help.

Chapter headings, TOC, Index – I have a book with a minor error in a chapter heading. I don't remember who introduced the error, but it was certainly my fault for not spotting it in the proof. I didn't even look at the proof, just approved it, in the theory that I'd seen it all a hundred times before. Same goes for the Table of Contents and the Index.

Picture Placement and Descriptions – Make sure that your pictures all appear in the right places. Depending on the technology used by the printer, this could be an easy mistake for them to introduce. Also make sure that the picture captions are correct, and proofed.

Proof in final form – Sit down and read through your whole book in the final proof or galley form. I don't care if you're so sick of it you want to puke. After a friend caught the header mistakes mentioned above and I had to halt production, I took the time to read the rest of the book and found a half dozen other errors. I also made a few "final" edits and probably introduced as many problems as I fixed.

Internet Marketing

When a new publisher figures out that marketing is essential to selling books, there's a tendency to jump into some form of paid advertising. After all, it feels serious to commit money to an advertising budget, it fits nicely into a business plan for those who have one, and most importantly, it's easy. In our experience, it's also been a waste of money. It's not always possible to assess the precise impact of advertising on your sales, particularly if you are actively marketing a title through multiple channels, so don't start off by shooting in all directions simultaneously. However, thanks to being a small publisher with a number of active titles and years of experimenting, I can say with some certainty what has and hasn't worked for us. Keep in mind that paid advertising is only one component of an overall marketing strategy, and it's a component that our case study title did entirely without.

Traditional Book Marketing

Here's the quick run down on advertising we've paid for. A cooperative mailing to the 3,000 public libraries with the largest budgets sold three books. This was a pretty classy mailing, nice envelope, nice stamp, only two other publisher fliers included with ours. The books advertised both had some previous success in library sales, were well reviewed, and were offered at a 30% discount. Publishers who do a lot of mailings will tell you that repeated exposure is critical, that content must be tuned, and that it's been a tough year for libraries. All of these things may be true, but at $600 to participate in the mailing and another $150 for the fliers, we have better uses for our marketing dollars. Displaying two titles at a major book show in a cooperative booth netted zero sales, but at $70 it was a cheap lesson. A small space ad in a specialty magazine, following an issue in which the book was reviewed, cost $144 and sold eight books. A paid link from a national religious organization's page for gift shop suppliers to an appropriate title cost $200, and in over a year, resulted in zero sales and a bare handful of visitors to the specific page linked. Subsidy published authors are frequently conned into spending thousand of dollars on small space ads in the Book Review sections of national papers, with zero sales resulting. The rule of thumb for expensive newspaper and magazine advertising is it's wasted money unless the author is famous or the ad can quote some superstar saying the book is a must-read. No amount of advertising can substitute for a sales force if your goal is to get your titles stocked in stores.

Free advertising has worked much better for us than paid advertising. Every published book review has sold some books. The sell-through isn't only dependent on the placement and tone of the review, it's also dependent on the availability of your title to the reader. Before switching to POD, we were bitten repeatedly by distributors reporting to potential customers that our books were out of stock and the availability status was unknown. Fortunately, some of our customers went to the effort of contacting us directly when this happened, so in addition to making the sale we learned something about the distribution channel. Book readings are an effective way to sell books, though the actual sell-through is dependent on the particular crowd. An interview on local access television stations produced no increase in sales. Free advertising also requires a sense of timing. We were thrilled to have a book excerpt accepted for publication in a national magazine with a circulation of over 100,000, but lacked the savvy to tell them to wait a year until the book was published. The result: zero sales.

When you write ad copy for traditional advertising and query letters for book reviews, treat it just like a book manuscript and put it through a proofreading process. Advertisements with mistakes in them are unlikely to sell many books, and nobody is going to request or read a review copy from an author who starts out, "Deer Surs." When you have an article accepted for publication or are interviewed by a journalist and are given an opportunity to look at the final copy, don't take it lightly. I once approved an article for publication where the promotional value was all wrapped up in our web address, which was spelled wrong! A tip for authors using a subsidy publisher, particularly one of the industry giants that publishes thousands of books a year by anybody with a credit card, is not to mention the publisher name in any advertisements or solicitations.

Review and Exam Copies

When you send out books for review, you can expect to see them appear for sale on the Internet, even if you stamp "Review Copy - Not For Resale" on the cover. Even worse, that stamp may prejudice your chances of getting a review, whether or not the person you sent it to is in the business of selling books. There's nothing wrong with reviewers selling books and some review publications count on book sales for a portion of their revenue. However, there's also no rule saying you have to send out review copies, and I certainly wouldn't send anybody a review copy without first confirming by e-mail that they are interested in seeing it.

A college or other academic institution may request a number of examination copies of a book to consider for classroom adoption. This is an accepted industry practice in which the institution gets 60 or 90 days to examine the books, and, if they order a sufficient quantity (like 10 books per exam copy), they can keep the exam copies for free. Otherwise, they can either return the books to you, at their expense, or pay for them at your academic discount. Just get the terms clear before you send the books, and check on the Internet to make sure that the school or institution actually exists. We've already had a college adopt one of our POD books for classroom use, and we set our academic discount to be the same as our 35% wholesale discount for prepaid orders. These transactions are entirely hands-off for us, as we have Lightning Source ship these books directly to the schools.

Internet Book Marketing

As of the beginning of 2004, our Foner Books and Dailey International (our offset publisher) websites combined for an average of over 3,000 unique visitors per day. That's over one million visitors a year. Each site has its own unique domain name, fonerbooks.com and daileyint.com, and each costs us $10/month in hosting fees. If you've written or have acquired the rights to one or more books, you already have the main ingredient needed to build a successful website—content. Nobody will ever give our sites an award for artistic excellence, but until search engines start accounting for aesthetics in their ranking algorithms, it's not that important.

The full draft of our case study title, "Start Your Own Computer Business," was posted online for a year before we published the book with Lightning Source POD. Prepublication sales weren't too impressive, but we left the whole draft online until readers started e-mailing us asking, "I've read the online version. Great book! Am I missing out if I don't buy the published version?" Our honest answer was that barring some editing, proofreading and illustrations, they'd certainly gotten the meat of this nonfiction book. Finally, one guy wrote us quoting a paraphrased section heading out of the book, asking, "Are you running a publishing company or a money losing hobby?"

At that point we took all but the first three chapters of the book offline, and sales immediately jumped by 200%. The moral is that you can't give away the whole book for free and not impact sales. Eventually we put short excerpts from each of the remaining chapters back on the website, and some of these draw ten or twenty direct visitors a day, simply because the tight focus of the subjects. In the early stages of a new title's availability, the majority of our Amazon sales come directly from our website. Once the book gets on the radar screen at Amazon through steadily growing sales, Amazon moves the title higher and higher in their search results, until significant sales are coming through shoppers who start at Amazon. This process can take from three to six months, depending on how many Amazon sales you make through your site and how much competition there is on Amazon.

To our surprise, the biggest sales channel for our POD books has been bookstore orders through Ingram, filling requests from customers of the chains, like Barnes&Noble and Borders, in addition to hundreds of independent bookstores. Recently, Barnes&Noble also began ordering directly from Lightning Source. We know the vast majority of these sales are generated through the website or word-of-mouth from previous website purchases, because those sales track website traffic and availability very closely. Some bookstore sales are actually generated by customers searching for a book on Amazon, and then ordering it through their local store if Amazon's estimated delivery time is a week or longer, or if the customer simply prefers purchasing locally.

Internet Reliability

The Internet has the same reliability issues as any other business infrastructure, with a few extra wildcards in the form of viruses and worms and spoofing. Everybody has heard of Internet viruses and worms in recent years, insidious programs that can find their way into unprotected computers and cause all sorts of havoc. The crude viruses and worms are easily spread by way of e-mail attachments, so the first line of defense is never to open attachments that you aren't expecting. This includes attachments from your mother or your best friend, because their computer may have been infected by a virus or worm that automatically sends itself to everybody in their address book. A fairly new abuse of the Internet mail honor system is spoofing, where the person sending out junk mail or viruses simply lies about who they are. If you start getting bounce messages (rejections from mail servers stating that your e-mail couldn't be delivered because the addressee doesn't exist or because of an embedded virus), and you don't even know the people the message was addressed to, you've probably been spoofed. There's nothing you can do about it, any more than if some stranger was sending out chain letters through the post office and putting your return address on the envelope. It's illegal, but try catching them. The fault usually lies with a friend, family member, or somebody else who happens to have your e-mail address in their address book and has let their computer get a virus.

Your web host (the people who rent you space on their web server) can't ensure 100% that your website will be up and running every second of the year. A good Internet Service Provider (ISP) will inform you in advance of scheduled down-time for hardware maintenance or software upgrades, usually a short period in the wee hours of the weekend. There are all sorts of other little disasters that can occur, such as regional power outages that outlast battery back-ups or physical line problems between the web server and the Internet backbone. There are some fairly expensive web hosting companies with redundant servers in multiple locations, but even these are no protection against the occasional Internet overload caused by a fast spreading virus or worm. I've found that the hosts who boast the most about their reliability also have the most problems and are the quickest to blame them on somebody else. About the worst thing that can happen to you from a business standpoint is to have your incoming e-mail disappear into a black hole, such that the sender has every reason to believe you've received it. This should never happen, but I've had it happen twice, in both cases due to the mistakes by employees of the ISP. Needless to say, I left both of these ISPs behind.

No-Spam E-mail Marketing

Nobody I know likes getting junk e-mail, affectionately known as spam. Spam is generally defined as untargeted mass e-mailings to millions of random addresses purchased for a few dollars over the Internet. Targeted e-mail campaigns to a self-selected group, such as the subscriber list of a professional organization or club, are generally viewed as acceptable in the industry. As a member of several professional organizations, I'm dead set against their selling the membership list to make a few bucks, and I eventually set up a separate e-mail account for those subscriptions so I could delete all the unsolicited offers without reading them. Despite that, if you have a genuine resource you want to tell people about, a website with serious content or the launch of a new newsletter, I don't think it's immoral to do a one-time mailing to a purchased subscriber list of professionals in your field. Just try to see it through the eyes of your target audience and don't send an e-mail solicitation that you wouldn't want to receive yourself.

There is such a thing as good e-mail advertising, and it follows the same model as print advertising in magazines. If you can provide people with actual content, articles they want to read, news blurbs or employment prospects in a specific interest or industry, even jokes or serialized novels, you can build up your own base of subscribers to a regular mailing. These opt-in newsletters are only sent to people who sign up for them and who can quit at any time. The best way to get initial subscribers to an opt-in newsletter is through an active website and high quality content. Organic growth can be very rapid since your subscribers will forward a newsletter to friends and colleagues if they believe it has merit. Nobody is offended by advertising in a free newsletter, though the positioning is a critical part of newsletter design. Don't load up the very top of the newsletter with ads, and don't place multiple ads between every article or news item. A single short ad at the top and the bottom is the classiest approach, and it should contain a hyperlink to a web page where readers can get more information. Don't use fancy formatting in a newsletter, as even the limited use of large fonts will be more than the e-mail software of many subscribers can tolerate. A slightly improved aesthetic is never worth losing a portion of your audience to software incompatibility

If you're looking for a quick way to get a newsletter off the ground, jumpstart website traffic, or promote a new book, you can purchase advertising space in an established newsletter. There are newsletters for every subject under the sun, many of which have membership lists in the tens of thousands, yet charge in the low tens of dollars for a small ad. Don't expect a huge result from paid newsletter advertising, that's why it doesn't cost much. However, the mathematical equation for launching a new POD book or Internet newsletter is less about making an immediate profit than getting those initial readers who you hope will get the word-of-mouth going. The best way to investigate opt-in newsletters for their advertising potential (not to mention news about an area of interest) is to set up a free e-mail account with Yahoo! or MSN and use it exclusively for when you subscribe to newsletters and professional organizations. It's easy to find newsletters to join on the web by doing a search on Google or your favorite search engine for **subscribe newsletter "topic"** where **"topic"** is a couple of keywords about the subject in which you're interested. Many newsletters will have advertising rate information included in every issue, and the rest will give the e-mail address of the newsletter publisher to contact for rates.

Discussion Lists

Perhaps the greatest information resource on the Internet is the discussion list or group, where people from all over the country or the world with a similar interests or professional goals join together to help each other. The downside of discussion lists is that when you're dealing with a large number of individuals, even if they all share the same goals, their personalities can really get in the way. There are professional discussion lists that are better known for their endless squabbling and name calling than for their one-stop shopping when you need an answer to a serious question. Personally, I don't join professional groups or lists for the entertainment value, so if the membership thinks it's a hoot to call each other names all night, I don't hang around. Discussion lists can be hosted for free on big name sites like Yahoo! or Google, or they can be set up on your own website with a minimum of fuss, as long as your ISP supports them.

The main value of these groups for a publisher is ready advice available when you need information to make a decision about anything from a new printer to a marketing campaign. However, there are also three ways you can advertise on a discussion list, subject to its rules. The first is by being the list owner, in which case you can do whatever you want. If list owners want to advertise a book or a website to their group, the usual method is to include a hyperlink in the group signature, the blurb that is automatically attached to the end of every group message.

The second method of advertising on discussion lists is through the e-mail signature of the individual member. If you're an active participant in a discussion list and you have a hyperlink to your website in your signature, people who respect what you have to say will eventually visit that website. Finally, depending on the discussion list rules, you can include an announcement right in a group posting, like "I just added a new article to my website."

In order to limit the clash of hundreds or even thousands of personalities sharing a discussion list, somebody has to be in charge of keeping order. This job naturally falls to the list owner, who takes on the role of moderator. There are a couple of different ways public list moderation can be handled. The most draconian is "full moderation" where every message is read by the moderator before being posted to the list. This introduces a big time lag in getting questions answered, puts a heavy burden on the moderator(s) and is a big turn-off to some members. Another moderation method is to set a relatively low number of posts, say three or five, that must be approved by the moderator before a new member gains unrestricted posting access to the list. The most common way to run a list is "unmoderated", which means anybody who joins the list can post whatever they want, whenever they want, within the list guidelines. If a member doesn't follow the letter or the spirit of the list's guiding principles, the moderator can and should ban the member, which removes the member's e-mail address from the list and doesn't allow the ex-member to re-subscribe from that address.

Private discussion lists are different from public lists in that members are added only through invitation or on approval of a request to join. While some people view private discussion lists as elitist, they offer a way for people to discuss subjects that they wouldn't be comfortable talking about in an open public forum. Private lists can also become necessary when a public list is too successful to meet the needs of a broad membership. This is very common with professional lists, where a mix of beginners and established professionals results in the same "how do I get started" questions being repeated over and over again by new members. You can create private discussion lists on the same sites that offer free public lists, it's just a question of the list settings. Private lists usually require less work on the part of the moderator and create a more supportive environment. Unfortunately, they tend to become so closely knit that some members introduce personal topics, as if they were having coffee out with friends, and it quickly becomes difficult to read through 20 or 30 posts a day in hope of finding something related to the professional topic. It can actually be harder to regulate these personal posts on a private list than on a public list.

List Moderation

List moderation is an art rather than a science. I've founded and moderated two good size discussion lists, one with over a thousand members and the other with several hundred. Discussion lists aren't democracies, and you can't count on public disapproval to keep cranky members from making everybody miserable. Members are welcome to complain to myself or my co-moderators directly, but I don't see why the thousand plus members who joined for professional discussions should be subjected to the extra load. Flaming, or saying nasty things about list members or their opinions, is also prohibited on most quality discussion lists. There's never a good excuse to insult a fellow list member, and I'll give one offlist warning to the effect before banning a member. List moderators also have to exercise some control as to when a particular discussion, or thread, should come to an end. Otherwise, members who politely and legitimately disagree on some point may repeat their points of view over and over until it becomes counterproductive. The best way to do this is to make an official "This is the moderator speaking" post to the list suggesting that the two or three people who can't let go of the issue discuss it privately. I strictly enforce a "no politics" rule on both of my professional lists.

I founded my first discussion group on Yahoo! by inviting a few people who had e-mailed me questions about the material on my website, and then added a link to the group from my website. It grew at a rate of about two new members a day from the outset, and we began getting fairly regular spam on the list, the same junk you'd expect to get in your regular e-mail. I immediately banned anybody who joined just to spam, though most quit right after sending the message. By the time the group got up to 500 or so members, we were getting spam every day, and I considered putting the group on full moderation so I could screen out those messages. In a last ditch attempt to prevent spammers from joining, I delisted the group from the Yahoo! public directory, and the spam came to an abrupt halt. It turns out that there are people who will go to the public listings of discussion groups, join any group with a large membership and start sending out spam. Delisting the group from the public directory didn't hurt the growth at all since the vast majority of the new members find the group through my website.

If you want to "capture" list members on your own website, rather than using a Yahoo, MSN or Google, you certainly can, but there are several benefits to using a public site. First, if the list grows into a useful resource, it's nice to believe that it will have a continued life even if you lose interest or get run over by a truck. A list on a site like Yahoo! will keep running as long as members want to join and the paid advertisements Yahoo! shows them are sufficient to justify Yahoo's expense. Second, many people, myself included, are more comfortable joining a list hosted by an independent party, rather than feeling like we're merely part of somebody else's business strategy. Also, the discussion list software used by a provider like Yahoo! will work on just about any computer in the world, with no extra tweaking or troubleshooting required on the part of the list owner. Subscribers can choose to receive every posting to the list, a daily digest, or special notifications only, and they can access the Yahoo! site directly from any computer to read the posts online or look through the group archives. Every privately hosted list I've participated in has had problems with archives, daily digests or web access to posts, and many of these lists were run by computer professionals!

Trolls and Lurkers

The worst kind of list member you can encounter is a troll. Unlike "flamers" who insult fellow members openly and regularly employ sarcasm and mocking to intimidate people who don't agree with them, trolls tend to be passive/aggressive types who try to provoke arguments while protesting innocence. It's a critical list management skill not to get drawn into public arguments with trolls, and I will quickly e-mail any new member directly and ask for an explanation if I suspect trolling behavior. If you're a member of a useful list, but not the moderator, don't try dealing directly with trolls or engaging in flame fights. Write the list moderator(s) directly with your complaint and ask them to take action. If they don't correct the problem, I'd suggest finding a more civil list or starting one of your own.

Most public discussion lists are filled with lurkers. Lurkers aren't bad people, despite the negative sounding name, though some people consider them parasites. Lurkers are list members who never contribute to the list, and they make up the vast majority of the membership on most public lists. In fact, the only lists you're likely to encounter where most of the members aren't lurkers are the private, invitation-only lists, some of which require a minimum number of posts for continued membership. Authors who participate on professional or publishing industry lists are sometimes shocked to get an e-mail out of the blue from an editor at this or that publisher asking them if they'd like to submit a proposal for a book about a subject they'd been discussing on the list. Yes, acquisition editors often lurk on lists, though how they find the time to read the extra e-mails is beyond me.

Amazon Associates and Marketplace

We've been members of the Amazon Associates program since February 1997 and it's been a model business-to-business relationship. Our only regret is that they stopped sending out free T-shirts in 1998. The Associates program pays website owners a small commission on the Amazon purchases that are made by customers who arrive at Amazon by way of an Associate's website. From the very inception, these commissions have paid the bills for our website hosting and Internet access, with our two websites currently earning well over $1000 a year from Amazon. Our participation increases the sales of our books in two distinct ways. First, it provides a reliable storefront that's just one click away for buyers who don't want to give their credit card information to just anybody. Second, every book you sell on Amazon helps raise your profile in Amazon search results, which creates a positive feedback loop, raising your Amazon sales rank and boosting your bottom line.

Some publishers prefer the Barnes&Noble.com program because BN.com stayed out of used book sales until recently. We're members of their program, but we've used it primarily for titles that get listed at BN.com before they get listed at Amazon. There are numerous other associate programs available from reputable companies for selling everything from vacation travel to advertising, but we've never signed up for any of these. The great thing about being an Amazon or Barnes&Noble.com associate is that it doesn't make a your website look like one giant advertisement, which is the quickest way to cause visitors to your site to leave without even reading a sentence. In fact, the existence of a link to these online booksellers helps to clue-in visitors in that you actually have books for sale, even if those visitors aren't online shoppers.

Paid Web Advertising

There are plenty of places you can spend advertising dollars on the Internet, some cheap and some as expensive as print ads. Generally speaking, I use advertising campaigns more to learn about the market and how demand for our titles is generated than to actually sell books. While Internet advertising can be implemented with a laser sharp focus that results in a relatively high sell-through, the cost for each successful impression, each time somebody sees your ad and clicks through to your website, can cost over a dollar in competitive areas. It's primarily a question of cost effectiveness. Since our titles carry low cover prices, we can't justify much ongoing expense for each incremental sale. The two primary services that publishers can use to advertise their websites along with search engine results are Google Adwords and Overture. Amazon has also introduced paid placements for both authors and publishers, which can give quite a boost to a title's sales, considering the number of books sold through the Amazon site.

Google Adwords

My favorite Internet advertising option, as both an advertiser and an Internet user, is Google Adwords. Google continues to focus on presenting search results ranked in accordance with their industry-best algorithm, which means you can quickly find the information you're looking for without having to sort through or skip by a bunch of paid listings. The small, almost elegant, Adwords notices appear in the margin of the page, out of the way of the search results. You might think this means that nobody ever clicks on the ads, but nothing could be further from the truth. It turns out that many people go to Google because they are shopping for something. I've learned for myself, when looking to purchase electronics and computer components, that clicking on the ads that come up is a more efficient way to shop than going to the web pages that appear in the search results. While the search results are likely to be right on target for the search term, it doesn't mean that those websites have the items for sale. My own websites come out at the top of Google searches for all sorts of computer related terms, but I'm not selling those parts, just offering descriptions of how they work or how to assemble or repair them.

Google Adwords has evolved over time such that it can be efficiently applied to even the smallest advertising campaign, simultaneously providing great insight into how people search for information. After signing up with a credit card, you start by creating a new campaign, which can contain different ads, keywords, and maximum payments. The first step is to create an ad of three short lines of text, consisting of an attention grabbing title followed by two lines (up to 35 characters per line) of detail. Then you assign the URL you want displayed, like:

www.fonerbooks.com

And the URL you want the people who click on the ad to be sent to, which may be much longer, like:

www.fonerbooks.com/book_title/adwords_campaign.htm

Next you provide the key search words and terms for which you want Google to display your ad.

After you save a list of search terms, you're prompted to give the maximum amount you're willing to pay per click-through, which I usually limit to $0.25 when I'm advertising a book. For less popular search terms where there's little competition, Adwords will often charge you quite a bit less than the maximum you select. The more you're willing to pay, the higher up the page your ad will initially appear. If there's no competition, you get the top spot at the minimum charge. Adwords also tracks the success of your ad and may promote it above other advertisers who are willing to pay more if your ad is more efficient. Simply put, if your ad attracts more people to click on it, it means more visitors for you and more revenue for Adwords than if they promoted an ad from somebody who was willing to pay more but whose ad didn't tempt anybody.

After reviewing your search terms, the estimated cost per day of the campaign, and deciding if you want to raise or lower you maximum cost per click, you set a maximum cost per day for the campaign. Adwords will suggest an amount that should guarantee your campaign can run 24 hours a day without stopping because the day's allowance is exhausted, but you can choose a lower amount if you want. Try to resist the urge of going to Google, searching on all your terms and clicking through to your website, or you'll be costing yourself money for no reason and impacting the actual data on how successful your campaign is, which is crucial for fine-tuning.

Example Adwords Campaign

While in the process of writing this book, we decided to run a Google Adwords campaign to test phrases for inclusion in the title. We were also curious to see if we'd be able to afford Adwords advertising for some of the key concepts once the book was available for sale. We let the campaign run over the weekend and into the beginning of the first week of February. The ad we actually ran looked like:

<u>Print-on-Demand</u>
A New Publishing Business Model
For Authors and Publishers
www.fonerbooks.com

The following is a tabulation of the results, similar to the actual Adwords report available online from the start of the campaign.

Keyword	Clicks	Views	Average Cost/Click	Cost	Avg. Position
Total Searches	51	3,847	$0.20	$10.20	7.8
Content Targeting	3	2,495	$0.18	$0.54	4.8
Print-on-Demand	21	727	$0.23	$4.72	7.5
Self-publishing	7	538	$0.21	$1.41	13.7
Small Publisher	5	226	$0.13	$0.64	2.4
Self-publisher	3	117	$0.21	$0.62	9.3
On Demand Printing	3	103	$0.14	$0.40	10.4
Book Publishing	10	1,469	$0.22	$2.11	7.2
Book Marketing	1	224	$0.25	$0.25	5.7
Book Promotion	0	205	-	-	8.6
Publishing Business	1	194	$0.05	$0.05	3.3
Book Selling	0	33	-	-	4.7
Book Business	0	11	-	-	9.0

From this data, you can see why we ended up using both "Print-on-Demand" and "Book Publishing" in our title. We also learned that with the particular ad we were using, that stressed print-on-demand in the headline, we could count on attracting a little over ten potential customers a day for just under $0.20 each. Even with the low positions our ad was achieving on our budget, usually appearing with seven other ads stacked up above us, we were drawing some interest. These are extremely competitive keywords, with some subsidy publishers apparently paying several dollars per click-through to be listed at the top. That should tell us all something about their profit margins when they reel somebody in.

Overture

Overture specializes in targeted placement of advertisements, in the form of listings on search sites and directories, and was recently purchased by Yahoo! which is expected to integrate their technology. Overture has relationships with most of the big name search sites, excluding Google. Signing up with Overture is simple and inexpensive, the minimum campaign commitment was $50 last time I checked. You start by creating a list of search terms you are targeting. Overture allows free access to their Search Term Suggestion Tool, which provides access to a database of actual search terms used in a previous month, giving you counts for how often that basic term comes up in different constructions.

http://inventory.overture.com/d/searchinventory/suggestion/

If they change the URL, just search for "Overture Search Term Suggestion Tool" in your favorite search engine. After selecting a list of search terms, you create the search listing or advertisement that you want to appear when your turn comes up in search engine results. Depending on the search engine being used, the paid search results may be the only results that most users ever see and click on. Overture sells that actual placement in an auction method, where the top bidder gets the top placement. Very popular terms will be too expensive for a publisher to use in an attempt to attract book customers, but more specific terms that may actually be superior for targeting a new title's market may be available for as little as a nickel per click. As with Google Adwords, you only pay when somebody actually clicks through to your site.

Amazon Paid Placements

Amazon is always working on new ways to allow publishers, or even individual authors, to promote their books on the Amazon website. The most attractive option I've seen to date is the sale of the **Better Together** place on the page of a complimentary or competing title. Originally, **Better Together** displayed side-by-side book covers of the title the customer was shopping for and the title past customers had most frequently purchased along with it. This approach had the dual benefit of increasing Amazon's chance of selling another book, while increasing the likelihood the customer would end up with two books that really were better together. Data gathered through our Associates sites showed this to be a highly effective sales tool, with approximately 25% of customers purchasing the **Better Together** title when the prices of both books were under $25 and could qualify for free shipping if purchased together. By this math, purchasing **Better Together** placement, especially pairing a new title with a classic in the genre, could really help launch sales and raise the title's profile on Amazon. However, this equation may change radically if Amazon changes the current format of their pages.

It's a double-edged sword for publishers, giving a publisher that is willing to pay for the placement an advantage over a publisher whose book may have earned the **Better Together** spot based on actual sales. At the start of 2004, the cost for a small publisher to buy the spot with a moderately successful title was $500 for one month. While the price compares favorably with the cost of print ads, it can usually only be justified in terms of building a new title's standing, as opposed to immediate profits. For example, if you purchased the **Better Together** spot for your new title with an industry classic that is holding a steady Amazon sales rank around 500, you might expect to sell an additional 100 copies of your title through Amazon that month. If your net is $5 per book, you're just breaking even. If the title you pair your book with has a lower sales rank, say in the 1000 to 2000 range, the chances of earning your money back that month are very poor indeed. However, the boost in your new title's sales rank may propel it into meaningful placement in Amazon search results and benefit sales for months to come.

When Amazon first introduced this advertising option, it was instructive to watch both authors and trade publishers experimenting with it in a seemingly random manner. Some chose to buy **Better Together** placement for dated books that had been cluttering up the warehouse, in hopes of jump-starting sales. This turns out to be a silly waste of money for several reasons. First of all, older trade books that didn't sell well are widely available in the remainder market and sold by dealers on Amazon. This means these authors and publishers were paying to advertise books that in most cases, even if purchased, wouldn't earn them any money! Another flaw is that a title that has failed to earn a place even in the **Also Purchased** list probably hasn't been selling with the target title for a reason, like they really aren't complementary books. Some authors and publishers also failed to grasp the free shipping part of the equation, and bought **Better Together** placement with books that simply don't qualify for free shipping, based on weight or size. Finally, I've seen **Better Together** placement purchased with titles that are only selling 10 or 20 copies a week. Even if this translates into a 25% sell-through for the promoted title, sales of an additional three or five copies a week for a month isn't going to do much to help the promoted title's sales rank in the long run, nor return a significant fraction of the promotion cost.

Amazon Search Inside the Book

When Amazon **Search Inside the Book** was introduced, there was an active debate over whether or not it would help sales. Amazon reported that early participants in the program experienced average sales gains in the low double digits, approximately 13%. My personal opinion at the time was that **Search Inside** would hurt reference books, since people rarely read reference books cover to cover, and looking up the information on Amazon would now be easier than actually buying the book and looking in the index!

After several months of tracking books from the original **Search Inside** crop, and watching the sales ranks of books added to the database, I concluded that publishers can't afford to ignore the program, and I signed up myself. The reason is that books included in the program end up being accessed more often than books that aren't in the program. This apparently causes Amazon to deem them more popular than the books which aren't in program, which gives them an advantage in the **Most Popular** sort. I've seen books with perfect key phrase matches in the title and very strong sales lose their positions at the top of Amazon searches to books that don't sell as well and don't include a keyword title match. The only factor these usurping books had going for them was inclusion in the **Search Inside** program. Since the **Most Popular** results are often the first and only search results a customer will see, publishers who don't join the **Search Inside** program risk losing significant sales to the competition. Amazon recently added **Search Inside** capability to their A9.com search engine. Google is introducing their own full-text search enhancement called **Google Print**, but it's too new to predict how it will impact Internet book marketing.

Maintaining Flexible Sales Channels

It's important to offer your web shoppers more than one way to buy your book, despite the obvious advantage of building sales rank at Amazon or making higher profit direct sales. The reason is that people like choice, and my experience has shown that your overall sales will rise when you let customers choose. The huge advantage of having your website as the focus of your marketing campaign is that you can change the sales links day or night if disaster strikes. Imagine taking out an expensive print ad or scoring a book review in a major magazine, either of which has to be arranged well ahead of time, and finding out on the day the magazine is printed that your distributor has dropped you. How many of those customers who walk into a bookstore only to be told "We can't get that book," are likely to try back in a month? If your marketing is focused on your website and you find out your distributor has dropped you, it takes two minutes to edit the page and inform people that due to a distribution problem, they can only buy the book direct for the next couple of weeks. You'll lose sales, but you won't lose all your sales.

There are some federal laws which require wholesalers to offer uniform discounts to resellers for similar orders. This doesn't prevent you from offering special discounts based on quantity or other mitigating circumstances, but it does mean you should have a set discount policy to cover all the possibilities. You don't want bookstore owners or distributors calling you to ask, "How come you're selling direct to me at 20% off and my buddy tells me you sell to them at 40% off?" We've been surprised to receive the occasional direct order from distributors we aren't affiliated with, or from stores such as Borders seeking to purchase a title that they could obtain through Ingram distribution. The reason (we always follow up and ask) is usually that Ingram happens to be out of stock and a persistent customer wants the book quickly, or company policy prevents ordering through Ingram if a title isn't in stock. Because these have always been single orders, we've been willing to ship them on trust with an invoice for our standard wholesale discount plus shipping and handling. While there have been some slow pays (over 90 days), nobody has taken advantage of us yet.

Website Design

Authors whom I meet frequently ask me to visit their website and give them a critical assessment. What I usually find when I go there is an advertisement. Why would anybody want to visit an advertisement? Who would send their friends to visit an advertisement, maybe with the option to sign up to have more advertisements sent by e-mail? Why would any other website owner link to an advertisement, and why would a search engine send it traffic? A website has to consist of more than an advertisement, no matter how elegantly or cleverly it's conceived. If you're a superstar author, maybe fans will show up to read about your life, view pictures of you and your family pets, sign up to receive announcements about your forthcoming book tours and love affairs, but the great majority of writers just aren't in that boat. The only way the rest of us are going to get people to come to our websites is to give them something of value, ideally something that they can't already find in a hundred other places.

Serious authors who make a living though their writing are always willing to invest in the required skills. They'll join writing groups and seminars to improve their technique; they'll hire voice coaches and train for public speaking to promote books through interviews and readings; they'll buy expensive subscriptions to industry publications and scour them for publicity tips and marketing clues. However, when it comes to creating a website, they hire somebody to do it, and beyond providing a two paragraph biography and some book titles, they won't even take part in the process. The only way this can work out well is if you hire a web designer who knows more about your subject matter than you do, and if that's the case, why are you the one writing or publishing the books? If you learned to use a word processor, you can learn to design a website, and it will be one of the most valuable skills any writer can acquire. If you get bogged down or absolutely refuse to try it, at least you should approach the project as if you were the design manager and you're hiring somebody just to do the dirty work.

There's no particular value in a website that nobody visits, so if you aren't willing to invest the time to make your site a success, you're better off investing the effort in traditional book marketing. You can build a website in a couple of hours, but building a successful website requires periodically updating or adding content and making design adjustments based on the actual performance of the site in drawing visitors and selling books. It's not a full time job, but you should plan on investing a few hours a week over the course of the first six months of the site's life, besides the time you spend writing new content or corresponding directly with people who contact you through the site.

Writing for the Web

When you're writing for pleasure there's no need to worry about who your audience is, but when you're writing for business the target reader is the first consideration. The vast majority of free-flowing traffic on the web is routed from point to point by search engines. We're using "free-flowing" here to differentiate between visitors who are up for grabs and people who are using the Internet to do their banking, access work from home, or visit their favorite news site. Search engines, in the best case, work like librarians blessed with x-ray vision. Not only can they tell something about a web page from how other sites link to it (where it's located on the shelf) and the page title (the spine of the book), but they can also see every word inside. Through a combination of good writing, clever titling and intelligent organization, you can eventually earn your share of traffic from fair search engines. Unfortunately, search engine providers are businesses and they need to show a profit. This means that the best search engines employ advertisements and sponsored links to pay the bills, and the worst search engines simply sell the top places in their search results to the highest bidder.

In the context of book marketing, the most important thing you can do is to make sure that your web content (writing) is closely related to the books you are marketing. The easiest way to do this without jeopardizing sales is to post extracts or chapters from your published books. However, it's likely that you'll see even more success with edited or expanded writing that targets the same audience from a different direction. This is especially necessary when you're promoting fictional titles that are unlikely to provide the information a web surfer is looking for, even if a search engine should decide to send them over. For example, if you've published a novel, the story will be centered in a location. Certainly the author will know enough about the location to write a few thousand words about it, something about the history, something about current state of affairs, what the local food and culture is like. Organized properly and with some links from local civic organizations, the pages will attract visitors who are more likely to be interested in a novel featuring the locale than the random sampling that even targeted advertising usually generates.

Unlike paper publishing, web publishing is flexible by its very nature. If you want to correct a spelling mistake, change something you said, add a picture, or even close down the site, you can do it instantly, any time of day or night. The two critical components for any website are content and contact. Content is the work you want people to read and contact is the means through which they can react to it, normally e-mail. Unfortunately, due to the number of automated programs running around the Internet harvesting e-mail addresses for spammers, it pays to create a unique e-mail address for posting on your web pages and to use it for this purpose only. If you think somebody is a nut case, don't answer their e-mail; nobody else does either. Online arguments are a waste of time, so if you find you're at complete crosscurrents with somebody in a correspondence, just let it go. Many people who surf the web are often looking for answers so, if you are writing nonfiction, you might offer to answer e-mailed questions on your subject for readers. This can take some time, but it will definitely teach you what your audience is interested in rather than what you think they are interested in, and this "hands-on" experience really carries weight with editors.

For example, back in 1995 I signed up for a $14.95/month Internet account with a national service. Learning that it came with free space for a website, I posted a short guide titled "Troubleshooting and Repairing Clone PCs" which I had already written for some co-op students I had trained. People who didn't find an answer to their problem but thought I might be able to help them began sending me questions and, recognizing that this was "content," I began adding a new question and answer to the website each night. This section of the site, titled "The Midnight Question," became the most popular draw during the years I maintained it and had a large number of repeat visitors. That original short guide and the material from the "Midnight Question" became the core of my first published book.

All journalists now depend on the World Wide Web for information, and the questions and answers I posted on my site brought me two generous helpings of free publicity. The first was a front-page story in The Investor's Business Daily which described me as a "Digital Age Dear Abby" and the second was an interview and link on the Dateline MSNBC site which sent my site 10,000 visitors in a single day. These cases may be extreme, but our websites continue to receive regular exposure in both online and traditional publications, including recent mentions in the New York Times and The Guardian.

Website Design

You don't need to know anything about HTML (Hyper Text Markup Language) or FTP (File Transfer Protocol) to design and maintain a website. Publisher websites require text content to be successful, and even the simplest shareware or freeware web page design software is sufficient to get the job done. Our two publisher websites are designed and maintained with a web page editor that came free with the first Internet service we signed up for in 1995, and we get over a million visitors a year. Sticking with simple web design software will keep you focused on the mission of your website, which is to attract people who may be interested in buying your books. A dazzling animation or an original musical score isn't going to attract any search engine traffic to your site or tempt anybody to pull out their credit card to buy books. Many web surfers disable the browser features that fancy websites require to strut their stuff, and I'm one of them. Publisher websites should consist of simple text pages that load quickly, provide clear links for buying books, and be organized so that visitors can find what they need. Photographs and drawings should be included only if they actually add something essential to the presentation.

Search Engine Optimization is the art of designing a website that will attract the maximum number of visitors from a search engine. Attracting the right visitors is even more important than attracting more visitors, so determining if the visitors you are getting are the ones you are targeting is a key benefit of website statistics. In the bad old days of the Internet, search engines were very unsophisticated and many unscrupulous people took advantage, no doubt the same ones who are sending out spam today. Simply repeating a key word or phrase over and over again on the page was enough to fool the old search engines into sending massive amounts of traffic their way. Search engine programmers slowly improved their algorithms to do some crude semantic content analysis, which helped eliminate pages that consisted of a laundry list of key words. An early attempt at the honor system known as META tags gave the page designer the ability to assign to the page the key words and phrases they wanted the search engines to index, but was soon abandoned due to abuse. The current site quality yardstick employed by search engines is how many other sites have links to it, but unscrupulous link swapping schemes will eventually force search algorithm developers to re-evaluate this measure as well. Search Engine Optimization consultants will usually focus on some combination of the schemes mentioned above and charge an arm and a leg per hour.

One very basic, though often ignored procedure in web design, is actually going to the website and looking at all the pages using a variety of browsers. In fact some people confuse the local copy of the website on their PC with the actual site on the Internet server, and therefore don't realize that they've failed to upload some of the graphics or other elements to their actual website. Some web page design packages use their own browser to preview or test web pages, while others invoke whatever browser is set as the default on the user's PC. Web pages rarely appear exactly the same from browser to browser, and there will always be differences between what you see on your design page and what a potential customer sees when they are using a different screen resolution, which dictates the amount of data that appears on the screen. Depending on the way your design software works and what settings are selected, a lower screen resolution can result in everything being crowded into a longer, narrower page, or in leaving your order link hidden off-page where it can only be accessed by scrolling! If the visitor is using a higher screen resolution, everything may stretch out to the right, leaving the bottom of the screen empty, resulting in a site that looks nothing like you intended. The bottom line is to build your site a few pages at a time and test the results every way you can. Don't invest weeks (or thousands of dollars if you're paying somebody) in a design without at least changing the screen resolution on your own PC and viewing it in Internet Explorer to see how it's shaping up outside the page design environment.

Google offers web users and website designers alike the chance to see how highly Google values a page through its PageRank rating. The easiest way to get this information is to install the Google Toolbar in your browser, which can be found through the Google homepage. The toolbar contains a number of useful features, but the one we're interested in is the PageRank meter, a green bar that graphically shows how Google values the web page you're currently visiting. Positioning the mouse on the bar will give the actual measure on a scale of 1 to 10. Try one of the key phrases you're targeting, and then visit the top ten sites that come up, making note of the PageRank, page title, and basic content. If there are a lot of sites with high page ranks (anything above PageRank of 5 is extremely good) that also have the key phrase prominent in the title, it's unlikely you'll be able to compete with them on that key phrase any time soon. It's also instructive to use Google to see how many external web pages link to the page, and you'll see how much PageRank depends on quality links.

The Online Sales Pitch

On our websites, our basic sales blurbs appear on each of the web pages associated with a particular book. There's a text link at the top of our pages stating that a book can be purchased at a 20% discount direct from the publisher. This link takes customers to a dedicated ordering page that includes pricing and a PayPal credit card link for direct ordering, a link to Amazon, and some text explaining how the book can be ordered through local bookstores. We always have a thumbnail (small image) of the book cover somewhere near the top of every page, usually the upper right-hand corner, with a few words below giving the price, as in "$14.95 from Amazon." For some of our books, clicking on the book cover will take the customer right to the Amazon page where they can order it, and we make our Associates commission and benefit from the tracking data. However, the customers for each book behave differently, and for some titles, we've found we achieve a higher sell-through by sending customers to the dedicated ordering page that contains all of the options through which they can purchase the book.

Many publishers believe that all orders should be funneled through a single ordering page where they can sell potential customers on other books. There's something to be said for limiting the number of offsite links (such as Amazon, Barnes&Noble.com or your credit card processor) from any given page, in order to keep search engines from devaluing it. It's also nice to have a single order page so that when you make changes in price or availability, you only have to make the changes in one place. On the other hand, over the seven years we've been selling books over the Internet, we've found that placing the ordering options right on every page increases sales. In addition to the single Amazon link and local order page link at the top of the page, we include all of the basic ordering information, such as full title, ISBN, number of pages and price, at the bottom of every page. This helps drive bookstore sales, and it works well with people who scroll to the end of the page to find out what the bottom line is.

Getting Your Site Listed

Search engines and directories, once very different beasts, have been integrated to the point where I'll treat them as one subject. Examples of these are: Yahoo, Google,

Altavista, MSN, Ask Jeeves, etc. In a pure search engine concept you type a number of key words into a box and the search engine returns some or all of the sites that contain those key words in some combination or another, depending on the search conditions you apply. A pure directory is a hierarchical catalog in which you start by choosing a general subject, like "Arts and Humanities," then continually narrow down your search in layer after layer of categories until you reach "Bronze casting techniques in Ancient Greece." The key is to get listed in the major search engines and directories, but not to get taken in along the way by an ad for a service that will get you into 1000 search engines for $19.95. The vast majority of search traffic is directed by a handful of search engines and directories, primarily Google, MSN and Yahoo, with the majority of free-flowing traffic currently coming through Google. Make sure that you submit to any search engines and directories that YOU use, and hopefully your potential readers think the same way.

Getting listed in search engines used to be easy. You'd simply go to the search engine site, find the "Submit your URL" or "Add your site" link, click on it, and provide your web address. Within a couple days or weeks you were up and running. Well, times have changed. Google still accepts URL submissions, but the best way to get into any search engine is to get a link from an existing website they index, after which they'll find you by themselves. Some directories only accept paid submissions or make it clear that your chance of getting listed is much better if you fork over a couple hundred dollars. If you submit to any of these directories, you need to carefully choose which category you want to be listed in (again, pretend you are a potential reader looking for whatever it is you write about). Free directories usually only accept one submission per website, so choose the page you submit carefully. Directory entries are handled by people rather than automated software, so only a small number of submissions are ever looked at. In that sense, directories are analogous to big publishers.

Search Engine Optimization

Everybody wants their website to attract lots of relevant traffic from the search engines, and some people, the ones who make a living by selling ad space on their websites, are happy to get irrelevant traffic as well. Unfortunately, the way Search Engine Optimization (SEO) is currently practiced, it's more about fooling search engines into rating a site highly than helping them send visitors to the right sites. As somebody who uses Google just about every day, the last thing I'm going to do is encourage people to try to trick Google into sending them traffic under false premises. If you hire an SEO specialist to help build your web traffic, make sure they explain to you what they are doing and why it's ethical. Search engine staffers are constantly on the lookout for scams to artificially boost the apparent value of a website. If they determine that your website is part of a link-farm scheme or any other practice they've determined is harmful to the quality of their search results, they'll remove your site from their search results and you probably won't get a second chance.

If you're absolutely desperate for a couple of links to get your site noticed, there are a number of ways you can raise your profile without offending anyone or risking censure. One way is to join a relevant public discussion group that allows posts to be read by non-members (including search engines) and give a brief description of your new site with a link. Don't go around spamming unrelated groups and don't violate the group policies, or the moderator will simply remove your post. Another way to get some initial links is to join a webring (www.webring.com), a virtual community of related websites. I've even come across people who've gotten the ball rolling for their site by signing the public guestbook of related sites with their URL in their signature. I've also seen people abuse public discussion groups and guestbooks to collect dozens or even hundreds of links to vault themselves to the top of some non-competitive search results. Aside from the moral failing, they're running the risk that some alert website owner they've pushed from the top spot will notify search engine staff that there's something fishy going on. It's also a lot of work to go around creating links to your site that aren't particularly valuable, except in quantity. A smart search engine gives much more weight to links from national newspapers, universities, or other top ranked sites, than to any number of guestbook signatures.

Page Title Optimization

Designing a successful website, one that is attractive to search engines and serves the visitors they send, doesn't require any tricks. In fact, the more sophisticated the search engines become, the better your website will hold up if you don't depend on gimmicks to attract traffic. The most overlooked element of website design is choosing the right page title for each and every page. The page title is the HTML title, the one that appears near the top of your page when you view the source code, as in: <TITLE>Foner Books </TITLE>. If you're unsure what your HTML page title is, view the page in your browser, and the text that appears in the (usually) blue bar at the very top of your screen is the page title. It's critical to choose the right page title because once your page passes the semantic analysis that tells the search engine it's not just a bucket full of key words, the search engine uses the page title to determine what the author is writing about.

Let's say you publish books about gardening and post a page about raising cucumbers. It will likely contain instructions about selecting the best seeds, preparing the ground, planting at the proper time, cultivating the plants, attracting pollinating insects, discouraging pests, and even how to pick the cucumbers at the peak of flavor. If you title the page "Growing Cucumbers," that's what the search engine will believe the page is about, and a phrase it will send you traffic for, all other things being equal. If you title the page, "Digging in the Back Yard" or "Helpful Insects" then that's what the search engine will believe the page is focused on. It's not that the search engine is ignoring the other text on the page, it's just that there are millions of web pages about gardening, insects and eating, so the search engine relies on the title to resolve which of these subjects your page is really about.

Here's where true search engine optimization comes in. You title your page, "How to Raise Cucumber Plants" and make sure that the keywords actually appear in the text, so the search engine doesn't think you're trying to pull a fast one. But don't artificially increase the density of key words on the page. It may be counterproductive in terms of search engine credibility, and you don't want the visitors you do attract to leave in disgust with the writing style. Once your page is crawled by the search engines, you can expect good search engine placement if somebody types in the query "raise cucumber plants." But there may be a problem. What if most people interested in raising cucumber plants type the query "grow cucumber vines," "cucumber gardening" or "how to plant cucumbers?" You increase your odds with a title like, "Growing Cucumbers - A Gardening Guide On How To Plant and Grow Cucumber Vines," but that approach can only go so far. Search engines will downgrade your page if you repeat a word more than once or twice in the title and dilute the value of the individual words in the title as the length grows.

One method to determine how people search on your subject is to ask your friends and family how they would go about it, though it's hard coming up with a way to phrase the question that won't influence the answer. Better yet, sit behind them and look over their shoulders when they try. Another method is to make educated guesses and experiment with different page titles every couple of months, monitoring site statistics to determine the results. The irony is that when you figure out a super-attractive key phrase for your material, you can be sure that 100 other sites are using it as well, so your chances of being at the top of the pile are better with a slightly more obscure phrasing.

Both of the paid Internet advertising options we discussed earlier, Overture and Google Adwords, are very useful for optimizing your page titles. With the free Overture Search Term Suggestion Tool, you can check key phrases to see how popular they were in searches in Overture partner sites the previous month. It's a quick heat check that will tell you if people are searching on "Growing Cucumbers" a hundred times a day or ten times a month. Google Adwords, for a small investment, gives you real time data on how often your target search terms are being used. If you sign up with Overture or Google Adwords for a paid campaign, you'll not only get to test key phrases, but you'll send actual traffic to your site. You'll probably find that most of the pages on your website can be accurately described by many different keywords or phrases. The feedback from your advertising data can go a long way towards revealing the mechanics of how your audience actually thinks about your subject matter.

If you have much more information on a web page than you can capture in the page title, it's time to consider dividing it into multiple pages with more focused topics. It works well with search engines, and it works well with readers who are looking for pretty specific information, like how to make pickles, and don't want to read several thousand words about cucumber farming before they get there. When it comes to selling books, a large number of short pages help to give the impression that it's better to buy the book than to visit and print each of the pages in hopes that it will suffice. The best part of breaking a large topic down into component parts on separate pages is that you can learn from your visitor statistics which subjects are the most popular. If you use this strategy with a draft copy or with articles that you're considering for a book, you can use the visitor statistics to help shape the final form of the book. We aren't suggesting you write a whole book based on visitor statistics, that would be like planning family meals around what the kids like the most and you'd end up with nothing but desserts. However, when you're publishing for a living, you better pay attention to what the public has a taste for.

Internet Site Usage Statistics

There's only one way to know if your site is successful in attracting and holding the readers you're targeting, and that's to watch the site statistics. Even if you pay someone else to do all of your web design, tracking the success of the website is your responsibility. Every commercially hosted website should come with an industrial strength statistics package, but if it doesn't, you can buy an excellent one for less than $30 from www.boutell.com. The function of a statistics program is to generate reports on how people find your website, which pages they visit, how many unique visitors come in any given time period, etc. There are more report types available than you can use or we can list, so we'll just review the most important reports below.

Executive Report

All statistics packages will offer a summary of activity for any period of time you select: a day, a week, or a month. The top-line figures everybody watches are the number of unique visitors and the number of page views. Unique visitors are distinct Internet Protocol (IP) addresses (every computer connected to the Internet is assigned a unique IP address) from which your website is accessed. Page views are the total count of how many times web pages on your site were viewed. Unfortunately, page views can also be generated in large numbers by the automated programs that search the web for information or e-mail addresses to harvest. The summary will usually provide the total number of files served, which includes every individual graphic accessed, and is worth watching if you're subject to a web hosting surcharge for a high number of accesses. A successful website should average at least twice as many page views as visits. Less than that suggests that your average visitor is leaving your site without looking beyond the page they arrive on. If you can get three times as many page views as visitors, then you're doing extremely well, and your site can be termed "sticky" in the industry parlance.

Directories Report

All computer storage systems store information in hierarchical structures called directories. It's no different from starting with an office, putting file cabinets in the office, having drawers in the filing cabinets, files in the drawers and papers in the file. The office is at the top of the hierarchy, a single sheet of paper is at the bottom. It's just a convenient way to organize things, as opposed to just having a mountain of loose papers in the hallway. If you organize your publishing site such that each book you are promoting has its own directory, you'll be able to use a directories report to follow individual books without needing to remember which file names or page titles are associated with which books. This provides a quick check as to which books are leading and which are lagging. Images should always be stored in a sub-directory, just to keep the main directory from getting cluttered. If your web design software also handles shipping your files to the server as most do, the directory creation process will be transparent. If you ship your pages to the server one at a time using an FTP (File Transfer Protocol) interface, you'll have to create the directories manually, in a mirror image of the way the website is structured on your local hard drive.

Entry Pages

The idea behind tracking entry pages is to see which of your web pages are drawing the visitors. Website owners are often surprised to find that their home page, the page they expect is the first one seen when visitors arrive at their site, is way down on the list. Depending on the site design, the majority of visitors to the home page may be people who see the publisher name somewhere other then online, then type it into their web browser. The top entry pages will be those that other websites have linked to directly and those to which the search engines are sending people. For example, if you have excerpts from every chapter of your gardening book on your website, you might expect the table of contents to be the top entry page. Instead, half the traffic might be generated by an excerpt from the middle of the book which discusses pickling cucumbers.

Exit Pages

An exit page is the last page a visitor sees before leaving your site. Exit pages provide a good way to figure out if your site is working the way you intended. Sometimes the top exit page might be a pushy sales page, but more often it represents the page that contains the information people are really looking for but not finding directly from the search engines. It could be that your page title included the key words "manure" and "nitrogen" while most people were using "compost" in their search term. It's even more likely that there are many websites dedicated to composting which have far more incoming links and outrank yours on search terms containing the word compost. However, once your other cucumber-related content draws them to your site, that's the page where they end up.

Referring URL's

Referring URL (Universal Resource Locator – the fancy name for the address of a web page) reports sort the results by the top referring sites overall and the top referring sites to each and every one of your web pages. There's even a report of sites that have links to web pages that no longer exist. You should check this report occasionally and contact those sites with corrections. Whenever you see that a new website has a link to your site, visit that page and see what context they've linked you in. Unless you're a mind reader, it's the only way you're going to find out how other people view your site. New links from discussion groups and blogs show up far more frequently than links embedded in a web page, which requires amongst other things, that the person linking your content has a website of their own.

Top Search Keywords

Here's where you find out which terms people are using in search engines to bring them to your site. Usually it will be a phrase containing two or more words, but if you have a unique resource, you'll occasionally see some incoming traffic on a single word. If you're getting a lot of traffic for a key phrase that has nothing to do with your content, it's worth re-titling a page specifically to get rid of it. In the early days of the Foner Books site, when the only content was translations of early Hebrew literature and there was little traffic overall, there would be the occasional visit from somebody searching on "naked children." This bizarre result was due to the biblical style of the writing, in which the author expressed absolute poverty of orphans several times with the phrase, "the children were left naked and lacking everything." If you don't pay attention to which keywords are triggering the search engines to send you visitors, you can end up having plenty of traffic and wondering why you aren't selling any books.

Example Visits

Trails followed, or example visits, show a random sampling of what visitors did when they came to your site. The trail starts with the entry page, then lists in order each additional page the visitor viewed during their visit. If the trails make no sense to you, it's evidence that your site navigation (the way you link your pages together) is awful. If you see long trails jumping between unrelated topics or hitting every single page on your site, it's either an automated crawler indexing the pages on your site for a search engine or some data mining tool. Example visit statistics also show how long each visitor was on your site, so you can make an educated guess as to how much reading they're doing on each page. Just keep in mind that some people print everything that catches their interest, so some of your most impressed visitors may view a large number of related pages in a short period of time.

Visitor Data

Here's the bit that some people confuse with Big Brother, namely gleaning something about the people who are visiting your site. The statistics software keeps track of which sites and domains visitors come from, unless visitors are employing cloaking software that renders them anonymous, which allows you to determine broad themes in the types of visitors your site is attracting. Is your traffic coming from educational domains, from government workers, from overseas? If the majority of your traffic is coming from Australia and you don't have distribution set up there, it's definitely worth looking into. If the majority of your traffic is coming from government sites and you're publishing anarchy books, you might want to start looking over your shoulder.

Website Redesign

Once your site is up on the web, you can find it in the major search engines, and you've got a few months of watching statistics under your belt, it's time to go back and start changing things. It doesn't matter if you spent months thinking about and studying the issues of page design, organization and titling, nobody gets it 100% right on the first effort. In fact, we have some pages that have been on the web since 1995, yet I still find myself going back and tweaking the page titles once or twice a year.

The absolute key to success in redesigning web pages is to make changes incrementally so you can tell what works and what doesn't. If you change all the words in the page title, rewrite half the page, add or eliminate outgoing links on the page and change layout of your site all at the same time, you'll have no way of judging which change had what effect. You can pat yourself on the back if your useful traffic goes up or cry in your beer if it drops, but how is that going to help you in the future? Make one change at a time, like rephrasing the page titles with one or two new keywords, and wait until you see the top search engines re-index your page. You can do this by checking the page title displayed with the results when you search on an exact quote from your page at that search engine. Then keep an eye on your visitor numbers for a week or two and see if anything has changed. Don't even bother working on your site around the holidays or school vacations, because traffic during these periods changes so much that you're likely to misinterpret the results. It takes a lot of discipline to follow this approach, and being as impulsive as the next person, I often fall down on the job and change a bunch of things at once myself. It helps if you keep written records of what you're doing, even if it's just to send yourself an e-mail saying, "Changed page X title from 'Nasty Moldy Green Bread' to 'The Invention of Penicillin' in first week of March."

It's also a good idea to experiment with different sales pitches, which doesn't depend on waiting for the search engines to revisit your site and note the changes. Changes that seem minor, like where order links are located on the page, can make a major percentage difference in sales. Unless you normally sell a hundred books a day, you have to give the changes a week or so for the results to be statistically significant. I've been fooled a number of times when a change was followed by a sudden sales increase of a dozen books, only to have sales run a dozen books below average over the rest of the week.

Another factor to keep in mind is that Internet years are like dog years, so one year in our terms is like seven years to a dog or a website. Things change that quickly; traffic patterns change; search engines rise and fall or change their search algorithms; other people or businesses create websites that affect the standing of your site in the search engine results. To draw a reasonable amount of traffic from a search engine, you want to appear in the top three results for a particular key phrase you are targeting. You'll still receive some traffic for the phrase if you appear lower in the results, even on the second page, but only from serious seekers. If your content is superior to the sites appearing above, you'll slowly rise up the list as people preferentially link to your site.

When you feel your site is as good as you're going to get it with the content you are currently willing to put online, don't hang up your mouse and ignore it. You can spend your weekly maintenance time exploring new discussion groups or surfing the web for related sites and asking for links when appropriate. With the meteoric rise of junk mail, it's become more and more difficult to inspire someone to check out your site. The only chance you have of getting a stranger to read your e-mail is to get their attention in the subject line, and "Hi, I'd like you to link my website" isn't going to do it. Read a sufficient number of their web pages to make sure your own pages are complimentary to theirs and that they actually feature outgoing links, then in the e-mail subject, refer specifically to something they've written. I usually go with, "Your article about X" or something similar. Don't refer directly to a page URL in the subject line as lots of automated junk mail programs do that. Similarly, subject lines like, "I need your help," or "Please read," are going straight into the trash.

Another way to generate high quality links is to submit publication quality articles to newsletters and non-paying magazines that post the articles on their website, using your URL in your signature. Some of these newsletters are distributed to member clubs and affiliates, which means you may get multiple links back to your site for the price of one article that you're still free to use yourself. There's nothing to be ashamed of in asking for links, but I never make a pitch "If you link me, I'll link you," and I turn down such requests. I don't believe those links count for much in search engine rankings, and links to a "bad neighborhood" can actually hurt your standing or result in your being dropped from a search engine.

Neither Borrower nor Lender Be

It goes without saying that plagiarizing material from other websites is both illegal and immoral. To my thinking, this includes the wild "editorial usage" you'll often see on the web, where people cut and paste a half a page from a website into a discussion list post or their own web page, in order to comment on the contents. A link to another website with a one or two sentence quote is fine, but for anything more, contact the copyright owner for permission.

When I come across material from my own websites pasted into online forums or lists, I usually don't bother pursuing the borrower because the context is obvious and the nature of the posting is temporary. The usual tip-off to these careless cut-and-pasters is the "Stolen Objects" report from you website statistics.

There are two ways to be a lender: knowingly or unknowingly. When I find out I've been an unknowing lender (i.e., ripped-off), my strict policy is to pursue the issue until it's resolved. If there's contact information on the website, a simple e-mail saying, "You're violating my copyrights under international law and if you don't remove the material I'll be forced to take action," works around 75% of the time. For the other 25%, go to a database of domain name owners, like www.betterwhois.com, and find out both who owns the website and who hosts it. An e-mail or call to the owner almost always works, and I've heard some pretty sad stories in the process, like: "The individual who posted that material on our website lied about its authorship and has been let go." I've also encountered students plagiarizing wholesale chunks of my websites for submission as class work, and I've contacted the school administration who are quick to take action. For that one-in-twenty experience where contacting the website owner doesn't work, e-mail the hosting service, who is liable for all of the material on their servers, and ask them to shut down the offending site. This has worked 100% of the time.

Borrowed material will only show up in your web statistics package if the borrower was careless and left in links to images on your website. However, there's a remarkably simple way to find out if anybody has stolen your prose. Search for a small quote from your main pages in Google. It's amazing to see that among the billions of pages indexed by Google, it's extraordinarily rare to find two writers stringing together the same four or five words in a row. Every few months, I take a couple of hours on a rainy afternoon to do these searches, and I usually turn up a few offenders. Even if a dumb kid makes a copy of your entire website, it shouldn't have any impact on the number of visitors you get because the search engines will value the original site, with its incoming links, more highly than the copy. Still, it's always a good idea to protect your rights, and there may even be some legal drawbacks to allowing people to reuse your work without permission once you know about it.

Just to demonstrate how easy it is to come up with a unique search phrase, we started with the beginning of the first sentence from an article that's been on the Foner Books website for over four years: "Imagine sending a query letter offering an unfinished manuscript to eight publishers and getting back four positive responses within the week." A Google search on **imagine sending a query** only turned up three matches out of the billions of web pages they have indexed. Adding one more word, for, **imagine sending a query letter** brought the number of results down to a single web page, the one on our website.

Concluding Arguments

It's easy to give advice and even easier to ignore it. If I followed my own preaching on writing for the biggest market, I'd have titled this book "Self-Publishing with Print-on-Demand" and exclusively targeted self-publishers, rather than trying to write for both authors and small presses. My excuse is that there's no one right way to do anything, and with several successful books working for me, I could afford to write this one to please myself. Still, you can be sure that I'll follow my own advice in the Internet marketing of this book, and since you're reading it, there's a good chance that the marketing approach was successful. Some of the subjects in this book, such as Amazon sales ranks, self-publishing and contract negotiations, have been featured in articles on my website for years, drawing over a hundred visitors a day long before I ever set out to write the book. I don't think I could start writing a nonfiction book these days without first seeing that level of interest on my website. It doesn't guarantee that the book will sell enough to pay a working wage for my time, but the traffic and the large volume of e-mail received over the years tells me that people are interested and has helped to shape what went into this book.

If you ask enough people for advice about an authoring or publishing career, you can be absolutely sure that some of it is going to be really, really bad. Some of the worst advice stems from the old proverb about specialization, "If the only tool you own is a hammer, everything looks like a nail." My main tool is the Internet, but I try to acknowledge that there are other ways to go about publishing and promoting books. If you encounter authors who have had great success with radio interviews or even TV spots, they're going to tell you that it's the only way to go. Well, I can't even talk coherently on the telephone, and I don't believe that authors should have to become entertainers in order to make a living. The strength of authors and publishers is the written word, and the Internet is the media most ideally adapted to the written word since the invention of the printing press.

Writing for a big trade publisher is currently the only model through which authors can become superstars, but you may need to get your career off the ground through other channels first. It's not, however, the only model through which you can earn a living writing books, and I know more authors who earn their living exclusively through self-publishing than through writing for the big trades. Only a small fraction of trade authors actually earn a living through royalties, and of those who do, many live from advance to advance. Trade publishers and their employees are not an author's friends, and trade publishing contracts should always be reviewed by a lawyer. It's bad enough to author a successful book and find out that you weren't fairly paid. It's even worse to find out that you've signed away your future. Don't accept broad non-compete agreements or give a publisher the right to future books under the same contract terms, or you'll find you've gone from being an independent author to a serf.

When you do solicit advice from fellow authors and publishers, don't be shy about pressing for details. Far too many kindhearted people are willing to pass along the name of a friend whose services they've never used. The most useless type of recommendation is the classic, "Everybody says that so-and-so is the best." In my book, there's no difference between "everybody" and "nobody" and the only thing you can be sure of is that "so-and-so" is a wonderful self-promoter. If you're told that a certain cooperative mailing is a great way to sell books, ask the person who's recommending it how many extra sales they can attribute to those mailings and how they differentiate those sales from their ongoing sales. You'll be shocked how many publishers don't have a clue where their sales are coming from. If a fellow author tells you that somebody did a great job editing their book, read the book and judge for yourself. The same thing goes for book designers, web designers, graphic artists, etc. If they can't back up the shining recommendation with an example, take it with a shaker of salt. Even if the recommended person has a measure of fame, don't take it for granted that the fame is well earned or that their skills are right for your project. Real professionals are never offended by requests to show their worth—it's the frauds who get all huffy.

The publishing industry depends on a wide variety of tools, from word processors and graphics programs to scanners and printing presses. As you participate in discussions about the publishing business, you're going to encounter a lot of people who will tell you why the tools you've chosen are awful. If you try to defend your choices, some of these people will proceed from criticizing your tools to criticizing your intelligence, your writing, and even your ancestry. It's not worth arguing over, and it certainly has nothing to do with business or artistic realities. My family includes a number of artists, and the sketches they draw with a pencil and paper far outshine anything I can produce with a full set of oil paints and a canvas. It's not the tools that count, it's the talent. A skilled word processor operator can directly typeset a book that will be much more attractive in print than a hack working with $5,000 worth of desktop publishing software. It takes a reasonable level of craftsmanship to benefit from quality tools, and very few people will achieve that level their first couple times around the block.

Inventory costs money to acquire, and it costs money to keep. Unless you live in a particularly temperate climate, you can't store boxes full of books in your garage for years and expect them to remain in saleable condition. Everybody in the publishing business is chronically cash poor, because it's all about working on speculation. Trade publishers invest money in advances, book production, printing and advertising. Self-publishers have the same expenses, except in place of the advance, they invest months or years of their own time. Putting all your of assets on one roll of the dice is gambling, not business. Trade publishers try to control their costs by cutting down author advances and royalties, outsourcing production to the cheapest source, even skimping on promotions and starting with smaller print runs. For self-publishers who do most of their own production work, the only place they can save money is on the promotions, print run and groceries. The Internet gives authors and publishers a way to save money on advertising and promotions, though it requires an investment in learning and time. Print-on-demand saves money on print runs, reducing up-front printing costs from thousands or tens of thousands of dollars to essentially zero.

Trust fund babies and prestigious publishers with backlists that more than pay the bills can afford to publish titles without worrying about who the market will be. For the rest of us, publishing a book without doing any market research is like sticking a pin into a map and trying to open a fish restaurant there. Most of the time the pin will end up in the middle of nowhere, a forest, a desert or a lake. Even if the pin lands in the ideal downtown eating district, there may already be too many fish restaurants, or the people living in the area may all be beef fanatics or vegetarians. Most people, even on Internet discussion lists, would agree that sticking a pin into a map would be a pretty dumb way to go about opening a restaurant. The same is true for books, and making sure there's a market before you sit down to write makes you wise, not mercenary.

Print advertising is for publishers who have run out of marketing ideas. Direct mail campaigns, usually the last stop before print advertising, are expensive in proportion to the number of pieces mailed. Most direct mail pieces and magazine ads are never even read, so they can hardly have a positive impact on sales. Internet advertising with Adwords or Overture is unique in that you only pay if you get a serious bite. You don't get charged just because your ad appears on a page, or even because somebody reads it. You only pay for the ad if somebody is sufficiently interested to click through to your website. Not only that, but you can start tweaking both your pitch and the audience you're pitching to within a few days and a few dollars of starting the campaign. Trying to fine-tune a print campaign requires many months and many thousands of dollars, and the result will never approach the precision of an online campaign.

There's probably a guy out there somewhere who prints and binds books in his basement with antique equipment and makes a living selling them out the passenger door of his Model T for cash. He can tell you that you don't have to sell your books through Amazon to be successful and that there are other ways to market books than building a website. His idea of print-on-demand is going down to the basement and turning the crank. He'll tell you that he's been doing without distribution for seventy years and sees no reason to start now. Amazon, print-on-demand, Internet marketing and distribution don't guarantee that you'll make a living in the book business, but they make it a lot easier to try. If you run into a jam and you're looking for answers, try searching on Google before calling the friend who led you into the jam to start with. As long as you don't break the law or order up several tons of books on speculation, it's hard to get into serious trouble writing and publishing books. So, do your research, give it your best shot, and please don't compete with any of my titles!

Your feedback is welcome.

The author is always interested in hearing about the experiences of working authors and publishers. Please send any questions or comments to e_foner@yahoo.com with "POD" in the subject line.

Morris Rosenthal

Printed in the United States
60015LVS00003B/64-78